Why Nepal Fails

Doing Business in Nepal from My Perspective

Santosh Kalwar

U

UNELMA PUBLISHERS

Published by:
Unelma Publishers
Nuijavuori 1 D 29
02630 Espoo,
Finland
email: unelmapublishers@gmail.com

U

UNELMA PUBLISHERS

Disclaimer

This is a work of non-fiction. Although the publisher and the author have made every effort to ensure that the information in this book was correct at press time and while this publication is designed to provide accurate information in regard to the subject matter covered, the publisher and the author assume no responsibility for errors, inaccuracies, omissions, or any other inconsistencies herein and hereby disclaim any liability to any party for any loss, damage, or disruption caused by errors or omissions, whether such errors or omissions result from negligence, accident, or any other cause.

First Edition: June 2023

Why Nepal Fails

ISBN 978-952-65257-0-9 (Hardcover)

ISBN 978-952-65257-1-6 (PDF)

ISBN 978-952-65257-2-3 (EPUB)

Dedication

This book is dedicated to all the young people thinking of doing business in Nepal or currently doing business in Nepal.

Acknowledgements

I want to express my sincere gratitude and heartfelt thanks to my publisher Binay Dutta for accepting the manuscript and giving valuable feedback by reading early drafts. This book would not have seen daylight without his fruitful suggestions and feedback. Heartfelt thanks go to Arun Raj Sumargi, one of the country's top entrepreneurs, for writing the foreword of this book. I would also like to thank Jessica Ryn, author of *The Extraordinary Hope of Dawn Brightside*, as she believed in the work and found many parts of this book inspiring. Finally, I would like to thank Nirmal Thapa, author and founder of Color Nepal for his trust and compassionate belief in what I am doing personally and professionally in Nepal. Last but not least, my sincere thanks to friends and family who have supported me during all these years.

Praise for "Why Nepal Fails"

A massive well done for all your hard work on "Why Nepal Fails". You have successfully demonstrated a tremendous amount of knowledge and insight about the workings of Nepal in such a holistic manner and provided the reader with so much relevant background. Your genuine passion came across, and I found so many inspiring parts, and other sections were quite heart-breaking. There is a brilliant balance between encouraging accounts of business and success, along with the discussions of the realities of the challenges.

Jessica Ryn,
Author of *The Extraordinary Hope of Dawn Brightside*
(Published by HarperCollins).

...a delightful guide full of important information for those of us who want to continue doing business in Nepal.

Nirmal Kumar Thapa,
Author and FOUNDER at Centre for
Nepalese Culture (NEPAL Centre)

Santosh Kalwar is a prolific writer.
Readers' Favorite

This is timely and good work regarding Nepal's current economics and entrepreneurial situation. I must congratulate author first for being able to write so many things in this short span of time and also appreciate his sincere efforts in writing the non-fiction.

Binay Bhushan Dutta,
Author, Publisher and Entrepreneur

Contents

List of Abbreviations and Terms

APP	Agricultural Perspective Plan
ASA	Air Service Agreements
BOP	Balance of Payments
BIMS-TEC	Bay of Bengal Initiative for Multi-Sectoral Technical and Economic Cooperation
BIPPA	Bilateral Investment Promotion and Protection Agreement
CIA	Central Intelligence Agency
CEO	Chief Executive Officer
COPD	Chronic Obstructive Pulmonary Disease
CSO	Civil Society Organizations
CBOs	Community-Based Organizations
CAGR	Compound Annual Growth Rate
DMEGA	District Microentrepreneurs Groups Association
ERMEFN	Eastern Regional Micro-Entrepreneurs Federation
EA	Enrolment Assistants
FGDS	Focus Group Discussions
FDI	Foreign Direct Investment
FNCCI	Federation of Nepalese Chambers of Commerce and Industry
GON	Goverment of Nepal
GDP	Gross Domestic Product
GNP	Gross National Product
HI	Health Insurance
HIB	Health Insurance Board
IT	Information Technology
ICD	Inland Container Depot
ILE	Institute of International Education
IDP	Institutional Development Programmed

ICFC	International Capital Financing Corporation
IGCSE	International Certificate of General Secondary Education
KAFAL	Kathmandu Finance Limited
KMC	Kathmandu Metropolitan City
LB	Local Body
LGP	Local Governance Program
LSGA	Local Self Governance Act
MIT	Melbourne Institute of Technology
MOU	Memorandum of Understanding
MCC	Millennium Challenge Corporation
MOE	Ministry of Education
MLD	Millions of Liters Per Day
NCP	National Coalition Party
NFDIN	National Foundation For The Development of Indigenous Nationalities
NPC	National People's Congress
NCP	Nepali Congress Party
NRB	Nepal Rastra Bank
NEPSE	Nepal Stock Exchange Limited
NCP	Nepali Congress
NGOs	Non-governmental Organizations
OBOR	One Belt One Road Initiative
PDDP	Participatory District Development Programme
PG	Partner Groups
PAF	Poverty Alleviation Fund
PCRW	Production Credit for Rural Women
PPD	Public-Private Discussion
RRDB	Regional Rural Development Banks
RAPD	Remote Area Development Programme

RMDC	Rural Micro-Credit Development Centre
SLC	School Leaving Certificate
MSME	Ministry of Micro, Small & Medium Enterprises
SME	Small and Medium-Enterprses
SFDP	Small Farmer Development Program
SFDP	Small Farmer's Development Programme
SFCL	Small Farmers' Cooperative Limited
SED	Socially and Economically Disadvantage
SAFTA	South Asian Free Trade Area
SC	Supreme Court
SGDs	Sustainable Development Goals
SADP	Special Area Development Programme
UIS	UNESCO Institute of Statistics
UML	Unified Marxist Leninist or UML
UNDP	United Nations Development Program
UNESCO	United Nations Educational, Scientific and Cultural Organization
UGC	University Grants Commission
UIS	University of Illinois System
VDCs	Village Development Committees

FOREWORD

I am writing the foreword of this great, insightful, and inspiring book, "Why Nepal Fails", so, as a reader, I am Arun Raj Sumargi, executive director of Muktishree Group and FNCCI (Federation of Nepalese Chambers of Commerce and Industry) executive member. If you google my name, you will undoubtedly see a list of companies my brother and I have established in Nepal. Some people call me "a man for family and society," and we have been fortunate to be among Nepal's top and most successful entrepreneurs. I love books, but I also love to travel because travelling is equivalent to reading ten books. I am an avid reader and read all sorts of books related to the economy, religion, society, and philosophy. In addition, I have written research-based articles for twelve years on the Nepalese economy in *Karobar Daily*, an online Nepalese newspaper. Some of the ideas from those articles can be summarized here as well.

I was introduced to Santosh Kalwar's work by Binay Ji when he bought me the manuscript of this book a few months ago. Despite Santosh not being an economist, I was impressed by his work and wanted to give my input on this subject matter. So, I had a few rounds of personal interviews with Santosh on the telephone, where we discussed Nepal's "economy" and "agriculture". Based on those interviews, here are some of my ideas concerning this crucial subject matter which Santosh decided to write in this book.

During 2046 BS, the economy was based on a "liberal, market- oriented economy"; the focus was on strengthening the national economy by adopting open-market policies, but it has already been more than twenty years, and we have not progressed so much in the economic front.

Our Nepalese economy is very complex and traditional. Many people and countries still see us as "poor", "unstable", "backward", "traditional", "conservative" and "fragile" nation. The government has allocated three major pillars: public, private and government sectors. However, none of these sectors is functioning well enough. The public sector has boundaries and limitations, and the private sector is in the hands of few. The government sector is fragile based on mismanagement and poor functioning of employees in the government sector.

You can take the example of South Korea and China and compare them to our nation. South Korea adopted a "mixed economic system" that included a variety of personal freedom combined with centralized economic planning and government regulation. They also had a "Miracle on the Han River", where there was rapid economic growth following the Korean war (1950 - 1953), transforming itself from a least developed country to a developed one. For instance, China, our neighbor, where they reformed Rural Economic Reform initiated after Mao Zedong, is based on a "socialist market economy", where one state-owned company and private sector exits in parallel with market capitalism and private ownership structure.

Also, the former prime minister of India, Dr Manmohan Singh, adopted very flexibly India's economic policies, which grew the Indian economy by 8-9%, which was a significant achievement and made India the second fastest-growing major economy in the world. However, compared to these policies in our nation, we have not been successful in adopting any approach which would strengthen and develop a sustainable economic development plan and change the daily life of ordinary Nepalese citizens (In Nepalese: *Gaas, Baas and Kapaas*).

We could also see one example of foreign investment bought overseas to Nepal. However, there is so much hassle one must go through to clear the amount that investors are reluctant and would never want to invest in Nepal. Although the government encourages foreign investment both as joint venture operations with Nepalese investors and as foreign direct enterprise investment shareholders, the minimum threshold is about fifty million Nepalese rupees, which may be a significant threshold for any investors.

It is a very well-known fact that a Nepalese businessman or entrepreneur must face several obstacles and go through and do several paper work to do or establish a simple business here, which the author has also emphasized very well in this book. So, a person who invests a small amount and wants to do business here has to face a lot of difficulties, and sometimes it may feel that the government is eying on your investment, return on your assets or money and can pick up on you or your business anytime.

I would also like to give an example of Vietnam and Cambodia; they started long after our country, where they adopted a mixed socialist-oriented market economy which has progressed very well and is better than our Nepalese economy. Moreover, Cambodia has adopted a hybrid economic system with personal freedom and a fiscal policy which has been vital for promoting economic growth, reducing poverty, and providing short-term stimulus. Similarly, the economy of Bhutan, which is based on agriculture and forestry, has boosted, and maintained solid strategic relations with India and is growing better than ours.

So how would we make Nepal succeed not just in terms of economic policy reform but in any sector? First and foremost, we must think about reducing costs. For example, if we will not give public transportation in Kathmandu, it won't be easy to reduce cost saving structure. Secondly, our government should initiate a policy where we will be self-sufficient in the economy in the next five years. Unfortunately, it looks like we are not moving in that direction.

An example is the Melamchi water supply project, which initially aimed to divert about one hundred seventy MLD of fresh water to Kathmandu Valley from the Melamchi River. However, it comes for a few days in operation in one government rule and then vanishes for several years in another government rule. If, for example, Melamchi is a broken project, then what would be other alternatives for drinking water in Kathmandu? Unfortunately, such alternatives are never studied. Undoubtedly, there has been a political change in our country. However, there has not been any change in our mindset, behavior, structure, and reforms on various levels of government. Therefore, it feels that only limited people are getting more prosperous, and the economy and monetary policy are not distributed evenly in the country. Lastly, you can also take the example of Thai Airways and compare that to our Nepal Airlines. For example, both airlines started during the 1960s; however, Thai Airways is doing a hundred times better than Nepal airlines in all sectors and dimensions compared to our Nepal Airlines.

In the case of "agriculture", I am the chairman of AEC (Agro Enterprise Center), the agricultural wing of FNCCI, which was established in 1991 under a cooperative agreement between FNCCI and USAID/Nepal. To expand and strengthen the market-oriented private sector and why Nepal's agricultural industry has not progressed much in driving agro enterprises, we have rectified AEC to AERC, Agro Enterprise Research Center.

In other countries, two percent population is involved in agriculture, and a hundred percent of people consume those produced by limited agriculture. However, in our country, more than 65% of people are involved in agriculture, and we are still unsustainable. Also, we need to determine why we must import foods and agricultural products from other countries.

In the last fifty years of agricultural education and development in Nepal, a farmer's education has gained power in the federal or provisional constituency (In Nepalese: *"Krishi padayo, kursi ma pathayo"*). Nevertheless, the traditional agricultural tools (i.e. Kutto, which is used for digging on the ground, Kodalo, a more extensive version of Kutto used for searching barren and making it ready for plantation, and Kodali, which is a more streamlined tool while searching for it pulls large hunks of soil from the surface and finally, *Halo*, which is used on the upper neck of Ox who then drives Halo with the direction of the person operating in) should be removed. Instead, more modern agricultural tools should be adopted as we will also provide our farmers with international markets from Qatar to Canada. (In Nepalese: *"halo, kuto, kodalo fala adhunik krishi lai samhala"*).

Also, how can we holistically make the entire process of farmer development cheap for the farmers and the government? How can we integrate various donor agencies and the monetary benefits they provide with technology?

Recently, we have been experimenting and sending farmers to gain trainees' experience for five months in South Korea. Then, when they return to Nepal with 1.8 to 2 million NPR, we ensure they contribute to the agriculture sector and utilize their know-how. However, we need to increase the production of our agro-products with high-value crops before our agriculture is sustainable.

Still, we depend much on rainfed agriculture, a type of farming that relies on natural rainfall for water. In modern agricultural techniques, one litre of water is sufficient for thousand square feet of land. Still, we are working on backdated fifty years canal project.

Currently, we are working on a "hundred agriculture farm" project where we will have an integrated farmhouse, and thousands of farmers will be involved in this project. Israel is also doing a similar project in India; about a hundred farmers are sent to Israel to learn new farming techniques. We are also directing the government to open several warehouses, at least one warehouse in one of the provinces in the country.

I agree and emphasize that there is enormous potential for agriculture in Nepal, as stated by Santosh in this book.

We can reach a negative temperature to favourable temperatures in a short time interval because of the vast climate variation throughout the country so that we can cultivate many different types of crops. Some corporate houses are also working on agricultural projects. Still, those will not benefit the country as they do not impact the general population except for appraisal and medals they gain from corporate social responsibility.

You can also see an excellent example of self-sustainable business practices in your home district, e.g., Chitwan, especially in the agriculture sector and poultry business. Similarly, as part of FNCCI work, we have utilized this concept of ODOP (One District, One Product) and OVOP (One Village, One Product). These concepts originated in the Oita Prefecture of Japan in 1979.

In the last few decades, we have imported Kiwifruit, avocado, and dragon fruit of a whopping 6.5 billion in just seven months. Recently, we have started exporting one hundred twenty tonnes of twenty to twenty- two species of grains and cereals to Canada. Also, we shipped some agro-products for the FIFA Qatar world cup 2022.

Our role in AEC is to work with FNCCI and the Nepal government on "connectivity". However, on Youtube, you will find thousands of videos of farmers and farmer communities in Nepal for views and gaining cheap celebrity popularity. Despite those celebrity Youtube farmers, we must reach out to actual farmers in the country and make them more sustainable.

After the COVID-19 pandemic, everybody has recognized the importance of the agriculture sector in Nepal, and there are more liberal viewpoints from the private, public and government sectors. There are new and emerging agricultural products, and we must bring those into the market with proper branding. For example, potatoes from Mustang, also popularly called "Mustang Aloo", a spiced french fries made with local spices in the Mustang region in Nepal. It tastes spicy and zesty and serves as an excellent snack. Similar examples include *"Thakali Masala", "Akbare Khursani", and "Bamboo Salt (Jugyeom)"*, but these productization ideas have not reached our farmers in remote villages.

If we can connect these product ideas with farmers, there will be no middlemen in agriculture farming in the country. So we teach vocational education to hundreds of farmers throughout the country by providing technological solutions, especially how to do agriculture on immense hectares of land, productization, marketing and branding. Recently, we have also started working with Dhangadhi, and our vision is to turn that city into a city of flowers.

If we can transform Dhangadhi city into a city of flowers, sending about nine tonnes of flowers daily to Kathmandu, we can be less reliant on importing flowers from Kolkata.

In summary, our farmers must leave the traditional model of agriculture, adopt the new modern technology, and focus on high-value crops, e.g. Kodo or millet (Paspalum scrobiculatum), which grows in the mountain region of Nepal. Also, it has medicinal properties, whereas it is super rich in fibre, reducing problems like constipation, bloating and stomach cramping. Similarly, Phapar or (Duckwheat) could be marketed and branded for high-value purposes.

In conclusion, I congratulate the author for bringing this topic to a general audience and my attention and allowing me to express some of my ideas here in this book's foreword. Like I said on the book cover, I would like to reiterate: *"Why Nepal Fails"* book is witty, ingenious, and a must-read by all young, aspiring, and future entrepreneurs of Nepal.

Arun Raj Sumargi
(Executive Director
Muktishree Group and
FNCCI Executive Committee Member)
Kathmandu, Nepal

PREFACE

I was against writing yet another book in this day and age when the book market is plummeting, especially in Nepal. People are binge-watching many youtube videos, Netflix and Amazon documentaries, movies and series. I hear from many people that it is a hard sell for authors who write in English in Nepal. No publisher wants to see manuscripts from aspiring authors who write in English. However, Nepalese writers who write in Nepali are becoming very popular; the likes of Buddhi Sagar, whose novel has become a bestseller, kudos to publishers like FinePrint publication, bringing a lot Nepalese talented authors and showcasing the works to the broader world. There are now many writers writing fiction and non-fiction in English in Nepal and abroad. Our screen time has been more consumed in smartphone and mobile apps, and most of our reading is happening either in some form of screen device or very hardly in paper format. Nevertheless, as a Nepalese writer living abroad, the words of renowned author Manjushree Thapa might ring some bell to us: "we carry Nepal with us always" wherever we live and work.

Coming back to the topic, and like any author will love to tell you, their book is very different from others as this is not a fictional work. Instead, this is non-fiction, a completely different genre based on facts, somewhat accurate figures and several references taken from notable books, journals and magazines of other authors.

I was a friend of Ujwal Thapa, who recently passed away during the Covid pandemic crisis. We were friends long ago, even before he was recognised in Nepal and through his "Entrepreneurs of Nepal" group. Back at that time, we had some informal discussion on how we could make an impact in Nepal, and he came up with the idea of "Entrepreneurship" and "Information Technology" and how the community spirit can be lifted. Many aspiring young business individuals will remember him for the Facebook group he formed, "Entrepreneurs for Nepal" and "IT Entrepreneurs for Nepal". After many years of gap and not personal discussions, one day, I came up with Ujwal's blog "WhyNepal.com", a title blog in which he wrote "*Why Nepal Fails* (repeatedly)", and this was after he read the book "Why Nations Fail" by Daron Acemoglu and James A. Robinson.

Ujwal's quotes from the "Why Nations Fail"[1] book go like this: "Institutions, which have opposite properties to those we call inclusive, are called extractive institutions— extractive because such institutions are designed to extract incomes, wealth and power from one subset of society (mass) to help a different subset (elite)."

He concluded and discussed briefly that Nepal is failing because of such "extractive institutions" designed to extract incomes, wealth, and power from the masses. And discussed briefly why we couldn't focus on economic growth regardless of any political ideologies, as stated in the quoted paragraph: "The fear of creative destruction (the change that happens when old is replaced by new through the use of innovation in technologies, techniques and events) is the main reason there was no sustained increase in living standards in Nepalis in the last 150 years (since the Rana rule)."

It was about ten years ago, and after reading the book and hearing the talks in the peer group, during that time, I never believed any nation could really "fail". So I started reading and writing journals on economic trends, what makes a country a successful and failed state and slowly gave up the idea of believing that any nation would fail.

Then a lot of things changed over time globally and also in Nepal. Occupy wall street, Black lives matter, Brexit, the Nepalese Earthquake,

---

1 Acemoglu, D., & Robinson, J. A. (2012). Why Nations Fail: The origins of power, prosperity, and poverty. Currency.

the #MeToo movement, our new Constitution, the Covid pandemic and now, slowly, we are going through some economic turmoil. If Ujwal had been alive today, I would probably have asked about his opinion through the exchange of private messages. But unfortunately, he is no longer with us, and his ideas, passion, active citizenship, and wisdom will be missed forever. Recently, family and friends of Ujwal Thapa have come up with a new book titled "Why Nepal"[2] posthumously. The key takeaways in his book are primarily three-fold based on Swarnim Wagle's book review assessment: a) humility, b) enterprise-oriented functional democracy, and c) action-oriented visionary. So, I started this book a few years back, collecting ideas and thoughts from various young entrepreneurs in Nepal. This book entitled *"Why Nepal Fails"* is somewhat analogous to those backdated ideas and attempts to provide a backdrop of the country's geographic, historical, and economic aspects from my perspectives and also from various young entrepreneurs perspectives.

I thought of doing a startup business in Nepal back in 2006-2007, where many engineer nerds would bring in their desktop PC and form a company where our primitive idea was of designing a website and building a web development company. After several weeks of discussion and get-together, the startup idea flattered, and most friends went abroad for higher studies or work. So, I was left alone without a startup, and that was my first failed startup business. Several years passed, and I started another company with a friend living in Nepal and was willing to cooperate on many fronts; however, the partner took all the capital I invested and ran away to Dubai. Finally, I thought of giving up. After several years, I recently started a new family company. This company has grown from one employee to fifteen employees and running smooth but with some hurdles. Charlie Munger quote goes on to say, "Those who keep learning will keep rising in life". Failure is good and can be used as a learning tool. I hope to fail more and learn more throughout this entrepreneurship journey. However, it is hard to sustain a long term business in Nepal, as I have learned, because of many factors I have personally and professionally encountered. I try to include some of my failures and learnings in this book. Hopefully, aspiring entrepreneurs can learn a lot from this book, build a better business in Nepal (and some aspects elsewhere), and eventually make Nepal successful.

Santosh Kalwar

Chitwan, Nepal

INTRODUCTION

Nepal is a federal democratic republic. A prime minister serves as the top executive under the Interim Constitution of Nepal 2063 (2007), and a 601-member Constituent Assembly is in charge of writing a new constitution. According to the Country reports on human rights practices, the abuses committed by the security forces (including members of the Nepal Army, Nepal Police, and Armed Police Force)[3], who were accountable for extrajudicial killings, torture, and arbitrary arrest and detention; the government's ineffective enforcement of the law, which jeopardized the freedoms of speech and the press; and ongoing violence and lawbreaking by illegal armed groups are some of the most severe human rights problems Nepal faces. Exceedingly terrible jail conditions, with much worse ones in detention facilities, were among the other human rights issues. Officials have occasionally invoked antiterrorism law to defend the disproportionate use of force. Police and government officials at all levels were corrupt, and the courts were still subject to political intimidation, bribes, and coercion. The government occasionally curtails the right to assemble. The government constrained refugees' liberties, notably for the Tibetan group. Statelessness was a concern, and discriminatory citizenship restrictions against women were a contributing factor. Many cases of domestic abuse against women still

---

3. NEPAL EXECUTIVE SUMMARY - United States Department of State. https://2009-2017.state.gov/documents/organization/186683.pdf

exist, and fatalities tied to dowries happened. Despite being infrequently prosecuted, violence against children was pervasive, and commercial sexual exploitation of minors remained a severe issue. Discrimination against those with impairments, members of certain ethnic groups, and those living with HIV/AIDS was an issue. Violence related to caste-based prejudice took place. There were certain limitations on employee rights, and child labour and forced or bonded labour remained serious problems. Human rights abuses still go unpunished, which is a significant issue. The government did not do much to pursue or punish those responsible for abuses, whether in the security forces or elsewhere. Investigations into specific abuses and legal sanctions for the offenders were occasionally carried out. Still, for many cases of abuse—including significant atrocities committed during the armed insurgency—there was a culture of impunity due to a lack of accountability. Military troops, Maoists, and other politically connected people charged or found guilty of violating human rights were not arrested as directed by the court. As a result, many armed organizations assaulted citizens, government employees, members of certain ethnic groups, each other, and Maoist forces, mainly in the Terai area. Although the number of occurrences decreased over the year, particular Young Communist League (YCL) members with Maoist affiliations were involved in extortion and intimidation. Killings, kidnappings, extortion, and pressure were committed by members of other small, ethnically motivated armed organizations. Numerous missing person cases were caused by armed organizations (mainly in the Terai region). Threats of violence were used to frighten journalists around the nation by armed organizations, criminal organizations, and political parties.

A report by Thomas Bell for Aljazeera emphasized, Nepal's failed development where he talks about how Nepal is one the best examples of failed development aid – and why the donors keep pumping more money in the country?[4] In Nepal, 16-year-olds are currently taking tests for the

---

4 https://www.aljazeera.com/opinions/2015/3/22/nepals-failed-development

School Leaving Certificate (SLC), or "iron gate," which will determine whether they are permitted to move on to - perhaps - more incredible things or lead lives of uninformed futility.

Most people have little cause for optimism—only 13% of government school pupils attended ten years prior and passed the SLC last year. The remaining students either dropped out or failed. However, since the 1950s, Nepal's educational system has benefited from technological assistance and international funding. The donors' much-heralded "School Sector Reform Programme", which is ostensibly building on the successes of the prior "Education for All Programme," is already beyond halfway through.

For more than 60 years, Nepal has benefited from foreign assistance, valued at over $1 billion annually and making up nearly a quarter of the country's total budget.

Decades of stunted development

Various hypotheses, claims, working techniques, and objectives have been established, discarded, and recycled throughout the years; nonetheless, despite occasional successes, accomplishments have fallen well short of what was once promised.

With "an increasing understanding of the need to adopt market principles," according to a 1991 USAID report, "we are confident that by the year 2001... we will see Nepal graduate from the ranks of the least developed countries."

Nepal currently aspires to leave the group of least developed nations in 2022. However, based on how things are going, it's likely to fall short of that goal, potentially joining Afghanistan as one of the final two LDCs in Asia.

What's at fault? War is a component of it. From 1996 to 2006, a Maoist insurgency murdered 17,000 people and hampered economic progress. However, GDP growth varied during the conflict within a range similar to before and after. Although there wasn't much infrastructure to begin with, it was destroyed, and most of it has since been rebuilt twice because of governmental corruption. Before the conflict ever started, village schools and health clinics were in equally bad shape as they are now today, over ten years after it finished. So Nepal had a conflict, although many Asian nations with more successful development have seen more significant competition.

Extractive government

Of course, the country's leaders are mostly to blame and have behaved similarly for decades. There aren't many politicians in the nation who can credibly claim to have taken "economic viability" (the newest slogan) seriously throughout their lengthy careers.

Instead, the government is managed like an extractive business, with the many parties and factions supported by a pyramidal structure of bribes, commissions, and office purchases. The education ministry, the university, the power board, the national airline, and the airport are formal public institutions hollowed down and left only partially functional.

In the private sector, cartels, syndicates, and "mafias" that control markets for drinking water, food, transportation, and energy, for example, receive political support from party bosses. Moreover, they gain from the disarray in the health and education sectors.

Despite the donors' claims that Nepal is "fragile," the way it functions and the people who govern it exhibit a notable degree of stability. Most have decades-long careers at the top, and many are the offspring or relatives of other influential people[5].

The funders are likewise mistaken if they think, as they frequently do, that the government "needs education" or "doesn't comprehend" what it is doing. The nation's leaders are influential in advancing their interests and those of their prominent supporters. Unfortunately, "progress" for the general public frequently conflicts with the interests of most Nepalis.

---

5 https://www.imnepal.com/reasons-why-nepal-not-developed-country/

Underwriting the status-quo

And yet the donors keep giving money. Recently, significant hikes were announced by the U.S., E.U., and U.K. In the meantime, as the competing political parties alternately quarrelled and worked together to split the profits, Nepal has fallen down the Transparency International corruption chart during the past few years.

In actuality, the government needs to be able to use the funding for development that it already has. A quarter of the money set aside for capital projects goes unused each year despite widespread mismanagement and a splurge at the end of the year that is timed to avoid scrutiny.

The donors are aware of this, yet they use budget growth and money distribution to gauge their performance and the advancement of their managers' careers. They strive to use their resources, just like the government does. Every year when the year finishes, there are hurried discussions in the donor offices about how to get rid of their unused money before the (increased) budget for the following year is due. (Apparently, the same thing also happens back home in headquarters)

Therefore, the donors are reliant on their beneficiaries. It would be easier to work if they began terminating corrupt initiatives or doing poorly. As a result, there are few instances of funders publicly supporting anti-corruption industries. As a result, the general public has a negative impression of government corruption and even corruption inside the development sector.

There is little evidence to suggest that the current crop of initiatives and programs will be more effective than those from the past. Many of them already have ongoing issues, including in the field of education. Few are genuinely new ideas.

The shoulders of giants

Instead, the contributors take credit for successes that most likely did not result from their labours. For example, remittances from migrant workers, which have increased quickly to be worth around 25% of GDP, are undoubtedly the key factor behind the recent advancements in poverty reduction. Nepali employees leave the country due to the collapse of the local economy. The money they send home is used to pay for private healthcare and education because the government-funded public sector is ineffective.

The development business has nothing to say about the accomplishments of the migrants and little to do with them. However, there are a few initiatives to help them.

The issue facing Nepal is not a lack of assistance or expert guidance. Politics is involved. And if the donors are to play a role in the solution, they must have the guts to demand real change from the cartels, "syndicates openly," and "mafias" perpetuating the nation's poverty.

Donors partly contribute to the sustainability of extractive politics by pouring money into the system without producing equivalent results. They should understand that even if a plan doesn't provide the desired outcomes, the money has nevertheless paid for something, such as the empowering of corrupt officials, increased inequality, and a decline in public faith.

They ought to be far more eager to stop participating in unethical practices and give an explanation. They ought to gather proof and present it to the authorities. Additionally, they must act to uncover and punish the misconduct inside the overextended and failing development business itself.

To do this, one needs to be ready to cut back on spending and accept accountability for what isn't working rather than just praising any improvement.

According to Human Rights Watch's World Report 2022, the government's inability to address the Covid-19 outbreak in 2021 contributed to Nepal's already problematic and uneven access to healthcare. In addition, government mistakes caused numerous deaths that should have been avoided, and an entrenched culture of impunity still violates the country's fundamental human rights.

Meenakshi Ganguly, South Asia director at Human Rights Watch, stated that "a lack of effective government leadership in Nepal means that nothing is done to defend individuals' rights, leaving millions to fend for themselves without essential services such as for health or education."[6] While this has been going on, "successive governments have declined to confront transgressions from the conflict years, entrenching an environment of impunity in which the police now routinely act outside the law."[7]

Human Rights Watch examines the state of human rights in almost 100 nations in its 32nd edition, the 752-page World Report 2022. Kenneth Roth, the executive director, questions the idea that autocracy is on the rise. On the contrary, people have recently flocked to the streets in great numbers worldwide, even in danger of being murdered or detained, demonstrating how popular democracy still is. Autocrats are also having a more challenging time influencing the election to their advantage. Still, he asserts, democratic leaders must work more to address national and international issues and ensure that democracy bears the benefits it has been promised.

During internal political strife in Nepal, when the government was essentially stalled by a conflict over the position of prime minister and frequent dissolutions of parliament, serious rights issues were ignored for months. Both of the Minister's administrations instead of employing non-operational and defunct transitional justice bodies to obstruct progress on accountability, Oli and Sher Bahadur Deuba, who replaced him in July, proceeded to impede transitional justice for violations committed during the conflict.

Senior health authorities reported a health system near its breaking point during a significant outbreak of Covid-19 infections that peaked in

---

6 https://www.hrw.org/about/people/meenakshi-ganguly
7 https://www.hrw.org/news/2022/01/13/nepal-authorities-are-failing-protect-citizens

May, with patients dying from a scarcity of bottled oxygen. In addition, the frequency of newborns in hospitals has decreased following decades of advancements in maternal and neonatal health.

In previous years, Nepal had made strides in eliminating child labour, but the economic effects of the Covid-19 outbreak, in addition to school closures and little government aid, forced kids back into the worst kinds of work. One of Asia's highest incidences of child marriage is in Nepal. As a result of the epidemic, many families experienced increasing hardship, and children were forced out of school.

There has been little progress in resolving the more than 60,000 abuse-related allegations filed with two transitional justice commissions throughout the conflict's 1996–2006. The Supreme Court ordered successive administrations to bring the law on transitional justice into compliance with international law in 2015, but they have not followed through on their promises. Instead, Sher Bahadur Deuba extended the mandates of the commissioners by one year as one of his first acts as prime minister.

The post-conflict Nepalese government's commitment to accountability and the rule of law has been undermined by systematic impunity for human rights abuses that extend to recent breaches. Abuse victims frequently come from underrepresented groups. Data from the Nepali police show that 18% more rape incidents were registered in 2021. Investigations were repeatedly unsuccessful, police were sometimes unwilling to file cases, and survivors had insufficient protection from reprisals.

The authorities frequently do not look into or bring charges related to reported acts of torture or murder by security services. In one instance, a soldier was convicted in July of Raj Kumar Chepang's killing in what is thought to be the first successful trial for torture since it was made illegal under domestic law in 2018. However, he was sentenced to only nine months in prison.

In order to achieve a high level of revenue and prosperity, it's essential to introduce new investments and enterprises into the marketplace. A greater level of investment is positively connected with a higher level of income and new jobs, demonstrating the importance of assisting new enterprises who are attempting to break into a competitive marketplace.

According to the World Bank's Doing Business Index (2021) Nepal's performance in 'Starting a Business' is in a poor state. Nepal is ranked 94th out of 190 nations in terms of entrepreneurship[8]. This is because entrepreneurs in Nepal encounter a wide range of problems while registering a new firm. Entrepreneurs are now unable to create their Memorandum of Articles and Articles of Association (MOA and AOA) without the assistance of a legal expert. Even though the MOA and AOA formats are accessible and issued by the government, enterprises cannot utilize them without the assistance of a lawyer or other legal expert. According to the World Bank, entrepreneurs find it difficult to avoid making mistakes while generating these papers without guidance.

To create these papers, it is necessary to spend NPR 10,000 and it takes five days: a significant portion of the overall time and expense. As a result, it is strongly suggested that the Memorandum of Agreement and the Articles of Association should be replaced with a single document that asks entrepreneurs to fill out essential information about the firm, its shareholders, and its aims. This has the potential to drastically lower the cost and time required to launch a firm. As it stands, the online submission of documentation and the subsequent requirement for the original documentation to be shown in person is excessive. This method could be shortened to a single step if the registration at the Office of the Company Registrar (OCR) were to be completed entirely via the use of computers. Nonetheless, due to a deficiency in the application of digital signature and electronic transaction technologies, it has not entirely digitized the registration process. If electronic registration cannot be implemented

8 https://data.worldbank.org/indicator/IC.BUS.EASE.XQ

immediately, the need to submit papers online should be phased out completely.

According to the World Bank, the incorporation fees in Nepal account for more than ten percent of the country's per capita revenue. The World Bank estimates that the entire cost of business registration is NPR 19,780, the same as the previous amount. According to the Central Bureau of Statistics (CBS), Nepal's Gross Domestic Savings (GDS) per capita is around NPR 15510. An entrepreneur would therefore need to save for 14 months simply to start a new firm. One of the problems in registering a company is navigating through regulatory hoops. As a result of excessive bureaucracy, the time required to register a firm has increased. Currently, higher levels of work must be carried out under the supervision of the same government authorities.

To access services from various government authorities, entrepreneurs must go from one desk to another to get signatures and approvals. Within the regulatory office, this has resulted in a labyrinth of confusion. As a result of the service delivery system, entrepreneurs must seek services from individual bureaucrats within the same government agency rather than from the agency as a whole. Because officials are in charge of delivering services, this has produced an environment conducive to corruption.

One key element contributing to the rise in the total cost of launching a firm is the centralization of regulatory authority. As a result, entrepreneurs outside Kathmandu must travel to the capital city only to register their businesses with government organizations such as the Office of the Chief Registrar (OCR) and the Department of Industrialization (DoI). The expenses paid in traveling to and from Kathmandu and the expenses incurred in accommodation during their time there contributes to the overall cost of launching a firm. These expenses add up to a total that exceeds the payments required for company registration. Firms, particularly micro and small businesses, are hesitant to register and run their operations informally. This is due to the difficulties they confront in registering their businesses and the many compliances that must be followed when conducting company operations. For example, there are tax requirements that are tough to adhere to, and this is one of them. There are three distinct kinds of income tax systems that may collect and remit income taxes. The size of the firm will determine the precise system that will be used. The existence of multiple systems can cause confusion, particularly for micro-entrepreneurs, who are neither able to understand which category they fall into nor which tax systems they are required to follow. They also have financial restrictions that prevent them from spending money on hiring an expert who can deal with these matters. The infrastructure necessary for the deployment of digital signatures, which is the most significant aspect in the electronic registration of firms, has been put in place at the government offices in charge of company licensing. However, many organizations do not have the adequate human resources necessary to properly deploy digital signatures and the complete application of electronic registration procedures.

According to the World Trade Organization, Nepal is a liberal country for trade promotion and an appealing investment destination for investment areas, investment conditions, investment incentives, and investment facilities. In other words, trade and investment opportunities in Nepal are safe and lucrative primarily as a result of the country's investment-friendly environment, flexible rules and regulations that are compatible with the spirit of globalization and liberalization, cheap labor, harmonious understanding between the government, employers, and trade unions, and free access to the vast Indian market for joint venture products. Nepal is geographically placed between two of the world's fastest-growing big economies: India and China.

The prospects of conducting business in Nepal are promising, especially given the enormous potential of these developing markets. In addition, Nepal has volunteered to serve as a transit country between its two neighboring countries. As a member of the World Trade Organization (WTO), the Bay of Bengal Initiative for Multi-Sectoral Technical and Economic Cooperation (BIMSTEC), and a founding member of the South Asian Association for Regional Cooperation (SAARC), Nepal is currently in the process of implementing the South Asian Free Trade Agreement (SAFTA). This would open up new avenues for investors in Nepal to pursue their interests further.

Agriculture and agro-processing, tourism and hydropower production, and infrastructure development are Nepal's most important development priorities. Additional prospects may be found in information technology-related services, biodiversity, human resource development, the education and health sectors, and pharmaceuticals, among other areas. The abundance of limestone and several other minerals in different sections of the nation provides opportunities for cement and other mineral-based businesses and the mining industry. The construction industry is thriving in Nepal, and there is tremendous potential across the board in construction- related businesses. Nepal has made a conditional promise to open up legal services, engineering, architecture, Research & Development, advertising, market research, courier, telecommunication, musical items, higher education, financial services, hotels, and restaurants, amongst other things.

The expansion of foreign investment in Nepal's sectors mentioned above is risk-free, secure, and highly beneficial. Nepal can generate 83,000 megawatts (MW) of hydroelectric power due to its position as the world's second-biggest source of hydropower. More than 6,000 rivers and streams flow across the country, with a total length of more than 45,000 kilometers. Nepal presently has a large number of hydroelectric projects under construction, several of which are commercially viable. Investing in Nepal's hydropower industry, which offers a consistent and steady supply of electricity to the local market as well as exports to neighboring India, is a wise decision. The trade agreement treaty with India provides considerable and favorable access to the biggest market in the South Asian area, allowing for increased productivity. Nepal also has duty-free access to the European market as part of the European Union's Everything-But- Arms policy. Because of the implementation of SAFTA, there is greater room for commerce and investment.

The current competitive industrial markets, vast natural resources, and varied agricultural output base give a plethora of investment opportunities that are mutually advantageous to both parties. Because of political instability and a succession of regimes, Nepal's transition from war to peace and democracy has been hindered. Although a new constitution was enacted in 2015, minority groups have continued to voice displeasure with revisions to the document that do not effectively address discrimination in employment.

Despite establishing two transitional justice commissions, they have not functioned with sufficient openness or followed international law, and victims and their families have not received justice. In April 2015, Nepal was struck by two terrible earthquakes that destroyed half a million houses and injured a quarter of a million. In the face of continuing denial of the right to proper housing, hundreds of thousands of people are forced to suffer both the monsoon rains and the harsh winter temperatures in makeshift shelters. Even though some restoration funds have been disbursed, the process has been very sluggish.

Hundreds of thousands of Nepalis travel overseas for work every year due to a lack of employment possibilities in their native country, particularly in the Gulf nations and Malaysia. Many are subjected to hefty recruiting fees in Nepal and are then subjected to forced labor, debt bondage, and other forms of exploitation in their new places of residence. There is still a lack of regulation in Nepal's recruiting market, which allows for the widespread violation of migrants' rights to take place. Because of the persistent violations of economic, social, and cultural rights, many people in Nepal are forced to live in extreme poverty, homelessness, with food insecurity and limited access to health and education services[9]. Child marriage is prevalent, and women, ethnic minorities, and lower castes continue to be subjected to prejudice and violence, notwithstanding recent improvements.

---

9 https://thehimalayantimes.com/blogs/no-place-called-home

Chapter 1: Overview of Nepal's Current Economic Situation

Foreign Direct Investment (FDI) can be a significant contribution to the growth and development of a country as it brings in cash, technology, managerial know-how, and access to new markets. Compared to other kinds of capital flows, it is regarded as a steadier form of investment, with the host nation benefitting in the long run. A 'one-window' system has been established to ease and promote foreign direct investment into Nepal by the Government of Nepal (GON)[10]. To attract the greatest amount of foreign direct investment into the nation, GON has implemented liberal foreign investment policies. The government has also been working hard to develop an investment-friendly environment to attract foreign investment and provide attractive incentives to potential foreign companies.

The Department of Industries (DoI) of the Government of Nepal is in charge of approving and overseeing foreign direct investment in the country. India contributes the most foreign direct investment to Nepal[11]. Enterprises operating in Nepal and other foreign companies have made important contributions to the country's economy, both in terms of job creation and the generating of income for the country's exchequer. Due to the proximity of the Nepali market to other countries, as well as the

---

10 https://mofa.gov.np/about-nepal/investment-in-nepal/

11 https://www.nrb.org.np/red/a-survey-report-on-foreign-direct-investment-in-nepal/

amended trade treaty providing preferential access to Nepali manufactured products free of basic customs tax, foreign direct investment in Nepal is particularly appealing to other countries.

Tourism in Nepal

Nepal's nature is in full bloom, and this is reflected in the landscape. Its majestic beauty makes it one of the most appealing countries on the face of the planet. It has a significant portion of the Himalayas. Nepal is home to the world's tallest mountain range, Mount Everest. At 8,849 meters above sea level, Mount Everest is Nepal's most treasured asset, according to some estimates[12]. As well as being home to the world's highest mountain summit, Nepal also boasts some of the world's other highest mountain peaks, such as Kanchenjunga, which stands 8,586 meters. Located on the boundary of Nepal and India, Mt. Kanchenjunga is the third-tallest mountain on the planet and the world's third-highest peak.

Nature in Nepal is not limited to the Himalayas. It can be found everywhere. Almost every aspect of nature may be explored in this area, from snow-capped mountains to the green rainforests of the Terai region. Mother Nature has lavished a dazzling array of beauty on Nepal's affluent landscape. In addition to being an environment controlled by nature, it is a country ruled by religion.

Nepal is regarded as a nexus for three religions: Hinduism, Buddhism, and tourism, all of which are found in abundance. Tourism is regarded as a religious practice in this country due to the variety of tourist attractions available, including abundant animals, historic sites, and unusual natural magnificence. Nepal has a plethora of tourist attractions that are second to none. As a result, Nepal considers tourism to be its most valuable resource. Its capital city, Kathmandu, serves as the nation's administrative center and is home to some of the world's most beautiful historical sites.

---

12 https://education.nationalgeographic.org/resource/mount-everest

Nepal has long been renowned for its historical monuments and stunning monasteries, and this is no exception. The monasteries have a great deal of importance in Nepal and across the world, especially because these monasteries are examples of Buddhist influence in the country. There is a devout atmosphere that permeates the monasteries, and the serene presence of Buddha can be seen everywhere. The fact that Nepal is the home of the Buddha ensures that Buddhism is the most widely revered religion in the country. The Buddha was born in Lumbini[13], another well-known city in Nepal, and grew up there. Aside from Buddhist monasteries, there are several well-known pilgrimage destinations. Kathmandu is also known for its magnificent temples, which can be seen around the city. Kumari Baha is a one-of-a-kind temple dedicated to the 'Living Goddess.'[14]

Throughout the city, there are further religious sites. A few of the most well-known sites are Bahai Temple, Buddhist Stupa, Hanuman Dhoka and Changu Narayan Temple.

In addition to its religious and spiritual aspects, Nepal is well-known for its adventure excursions. It is the most sought-after destination for adventure seekers because of its diverse landscape. Mountain climbing, mountain biking, rafting, and other challenging activities draw visitors from all over the globe to this destination. It is the ideal location for anyone seeking adventure in the great outdoors. Amid breathtaking natural beauty, adventure activities prove to be the best way to spend a memorable vacation with your family and friends. Already, tourism has played a significant part in the development of Nepal's economy. It continues to be one of the most promising areas for attracting foreign direct investment (FDI) due to the unequaled natural resources, holy sites, and treatments available in the nation. The Government of the Republic

---

13 https://whc.unesco.org/en/list/666/
14 https://www.npr.org/sections/parallels/2015/05/28/410074105/the-very-strange-life-of-nepals- child-goddess

of Nepal acknowledges the importance of tourism in the growth of the country's economy[15].

Tourism has always been a highly important industry in the country's economy, providing a large quantity of foreign cash and contributing considerably to its growth. Given its diverse geographical characteristics, ranging from the snow-capped Himalayas to wildlife reserves and beautiful valleys and its rich cultural legacy, Nepal provides travelers with a wide range of services, including adventure tourism, eco-tourism, religious tourism, among others. The government has established a flexible tourism development strategy to attract a higher number of visitors. By combining the natural landscape and trekking with other activities like rafting, yoga, and meditation, Nepal is developing its brand of eco-tourism. Investors in these and related services are encouraged to set up shop in Nepal.

Nepal is wealthy in terms of natural and cultural resources, and international investors may use these resources to make significant profits. The country's climate varies from tropical to subarctic in a very small area that spans north-south and is less than 250 kilometers wide at its broadest point. A big part of the reason for the high potential of herbs and herbal products is the perfect growth conditions found in the hills and mountains of the world. Nepal is home to hundreds of medicinal and aromatic plants, many indigenous to the country. Increasing demand for herbal-based cosmetics and health-related goods is being seen in significant markets like India and other Asian, European, and Western nations. Because cultivation and processing are presently restricted in Nepal, most of the country's medicinal and aromatic plants are traded in their raw form.

Investment in hydropower is one of the most profitable sectors for foreign investors in Nepal. The country's hydroelectric potential is

---

15 https://www.nrb.org.np/contents/uploads/2019/12/NRB_Economic_Review-Vol_23-2_Octo- ber_20112_Tourism_and_Economic_Growth_in_NepalBishnu-Prasad-Gautam-Ph.D..pdf

projected to be 83,000 megawatts (MW), with 44,000 megawatts (MW) assessed to be economically viable[16]. There is currently a substantial amount of foreign direct investment (FDI) in hydropower in Nepal, and more is likely to come because India has a large electricity market. The development of hydropower resources and the production of electricity for export provides the opportunity for the expansion of energy-intensive industrial operations. The potential for more than a half-dozen medium and large hydropower projects has been found via preliminary research[17]. Some projects are so large that their greatest value to Nepal will come from the prospect of exporting hydroelectric electricity to neighboring nations rather than from any other source. In addition to generating electricity, several of the projects proposed have the potential to provide huge advantages in irrigation, flood control, and inland transportation that extend far beyond the borders of Nepal. When the World Trade Organization (WTO) adopted the language of the Protocol for Nepal's entrance into this global trade organization, it was a resounding success[18]. Nepal was behind Cambodia as the second Least Developed Country (LDC) to become a member of the World Trade Organization (WTO)[19] after completing the whole working party procedure. As a result of this, Nepal may now fully enjoy the rights granted to all members of the World Trade Organization (WTO). The advantages are included in previous global trade reforms, which have resulted in an improvement in the domestic trade policymaking process as well as assisting exporters in competing in the global market and complementing privileged access to foreign markets.

These advantages will aid Nepal in its efforts to integrate itself into the global economy more effectively. India and Nepal are projected to benefit from signing a revamped trade deal, which would offer an

---

16 https://www.nbr.org/publication/balanced-hydropower-development-in-nepal/
17 https://www.nrb.org.np/contents/uploads/2021/09/vol18_art4.pdf
18 https://www.wto.org/english/thewto_e/countries_e/nepal_e.htm
19 "Serbia : Fabrizi Praises Reforms in Economy." MENA Report, Albawaba (London) Ltd., Sept. 2017.

additional boost to the increasing Indo-Nepal commerce. In addition, the new treaty is projected to enable more access for Nepalese exports into India while also strengthening and expanding bilateral trade between the two nations. The treaty's seven-year validity period is anticipated to offer a more stable environment for bilateral trade and encourage investment in Nepal due to preferential access granted to Nepalese goods under the terms of the agreement. Nepalese goods that do not meet the preferential access requirements might benefit from the treaty's MFN (most-favored- nation treatment) access to other countries' markets under the terms of the agreement. In addition to that, zero-tariff treatment for goods from Least Developed Country (LDC) is predicted to improve bilateral trade free access to Nepalese products in both developing and developed countries, making Nepal a more attractive location for international investment.

According to United Nations Conference on Trade and Development (UNCTAD) research, when it comes to profitability, the data shows that the rate of return on foreign direct investment (FDI) in less-developed countries (LDCs) is frequently substantially greater than the rate of return on investment in developed nations or rising economies[20]. These investors may reap the benefits of being among the first to invest. In contrast to regions where everyone wants to invest, early movers have the advantage of selecting the most attractive prospects. As long as they can handle the difficulties of conducting business in developing countries, investors will find their experience profitable.

1.2 Nepal: A Country Profile

Nepal features an astonishing range of cultures and landscapes within its short bounds, including the birthplace of the Buddha, the home of the Gurkhas, the roof of the world, and the country of mythology and beauty. There is no other place on the planet with such a diverse range of landscapes contained inside such a small geographical space as Nepal.

---

20 https://unctad.org/topic/investment/world-investment-report

The subtropical plains of the Terai, the temperate Himalayan 'foothills' of the Churia and Mahabharat ranges, and the high Himalayan peaks themselves are all included within a cross-section of fewer than 200 kilometers in length from north to south. More than half of the nation is more than 3,000 meters above sea level, roughly a quarter is at altitudes of around 3,000 meters, and less than a fifth is below 300 meters above sea level. Nepal is a tiny nation, yet it is the tallest country on the planet[21].

Mountains encompass 80 percent of Nepal's geographical area, posing significant obstacles in a nation where 80 percent rely on agriculture.

Nepal stretches for around 800 kilometers east-west and 230 kilometers north-south at its broadest point, covering a total area of approximately 147,181 square kilometers. Despite the tiny size of the territory, it has the biggest variety of height on the planet, beginning with the Terai, which is barely 100 meters or so above sea level, and ending with the summit of Mount Everest (8,848 meters), which is the world's highest peak[22]. Nepal is home to more than 6500 known species of trees, shrubs, and wildflowers, according to the International Union of Botanical Sciences[23]. Nepal is home to over 245 plant species that are unique to the country.

One hundred eighteen ecosystems, 75 kinds of flora, and 35 forest types. Nepal is well-known for its forests that draw biologists and geologists to research and study in the country's woods. Nepal hosts over 850 bird species (almost 10% of the world's species) and 181 mammal species, with over 850 bird species accounting for nearly 10% of the world's species[24]. The country's geographic location mostly determines the distribution of ethnic groups in the nation.

Nepal's population, which totaled a little over 23 million people in 2018, is mostly Indo-Aryan in origin, with the remaining 20 percent of the population being of Tibetan descent[25]. The latter group includes not

21 https://kids.nationalgeographic.com/geography/countries/article/nepal
22 https://www.britannica.com/place/Mount-Everest
23 https://pubmed.ncbi.nlm.nih.gov/31453417/
24 https://www.ntnc.org.np/thematic-area/species
25 https://worldpopulationreview.com/countries/nepal-population

only the Tibetan and inhabitants of North Nepal (such as the Sherpa, the Thakalis, and the Mustang), but also the related mongoloid inhabitants of the central belt, such as the Newar, Tamang's, Rai, Limbus, Sunuwar, Magar's, and Gurung people. The Tibetan and Burmese inhabitants of North Nepal (such as the Sherpa) depend on how precise the differences are made. Nepal's numerous ethnic groups speak anywhere between 24 and 100 different languages and dialects. Nepali serves as the primary language of the country.

Nepal was off-limits to foreign tourists until 1951, which contributed significantly to the country's mystique in the western world[26]. Since then, this tiny, compassionate country has grown in popularity among tourists seeking both physical difficulties and spiritual enlightenment in the mountains.

A geographical division may be made in Nepal into three geographic areas, each of which stretches from east to west throughout the nation. The Terai, India's southernmost strip of land, is bound to the north by the Himalayan foothills and to the south by the Ganges River[27], which runs through it. The land was covered with tropical flora; however, it has since been nearly entirely transformed by agricultural cultivation. The Terai region of Nepal is today known as the country's breadbasket[28], and it is covered with farmland. Central Nepal is dominated by the Mahabharat Chain, a group of mountains that rise to moderate elevations of 2,000- 3,000 meters, forming the heart of the country[29].

Rice, maize, and wheat are grown on terraced farms in the region, making farming a significant economic activity. It is in the Kathmandu Valley, a stretch of lush greenery smack in the heart of the Mahabharat, where Nepal's capital and other ancient cities are located. Eight of the

---

26 https://www.researchgate.net/publication/359625023_The_Quest_for_Sustainable_

Tour- ism_in_Nepal

27 An Introduction to Nepal - Geographia. http://www.geographia.com/nepal/

28 https://www.forestrynepal.org/the-terai-region-of-nepal-the-breadbasket-of-the-country/

29 https://www.nnmga.org/about-nepal/

world's ten tallest peaks are situated here[30], and the majority of them are covered in permanent snowfields. The region is sparsely inhabited, with minimal vegetation above the tree lines and there is little wildlife in general (4,200 meters). The climate changes significantly depending on altitude. The monsoon season lasts from May to October, during which time rain soaks the Terai and snow falls on the Himalayan peaks. Peak climbing weather occurs between mid-October and mid-December as there are clear skies and bright sunshine, with temperatures ranging from warm in the lowlands to crisp in the mountains, and the temperatures in the lowlands and mountains are similar. March and April are also suitable months for mountain hikes, while temperatures in Kathmandu and the Terai tend to be hot and humid at that time of the year.

Nepal, a nation in Asia's mid-Himalayan region, has borders with India on the south, east, and west and with China on the north. Because it is a landlocked nation, the nearest point of sea access is around 1,150 kilometers away. Geographically, the nation is separated into three ecologically distinct sections that run east to west: the mountains, the hills, and the Terai[31]. The mountain range is a popular tourist destination at an elevation ranging from 4,877 meters to 8,848 meters above sea level[32]. In terms of land area, it accounts for 15% of Nepal's total land area. This area contains most of the world's tallest snow-capped mountains, including the world's highest peak, Mt. Everest (Mt. Sagarmatha), which is the highest point on the planet. Located between altitudes ranging from 610 meters to 4,877 meters above sea level, the hills constitute the central portion of the country, accounting for 64 percent of the total land area. This area is home to various picturesque valleys, basins, lakes, and mountains. The Terai region is a low, flat area of terrain that runs along the

---

30 https://www.thirdrockadventures.com/blog/8-world%27s-highest-mountains-in-nepal-over- 8000m

31 https://www.world-travel-info.net/country/country/86/nepal

32 Kathmandu Valley, Nepal Disaster Risk Management Profile.
https://flagship2.nrrc.org.np/
sites/default/files/knowledge/Kathmandu%20Valley%20DRM%20Profile%202005.
pdf

country's southernmost border with India. This region has the majority of the country's rich plains as well as its extensive forest cover. It accounts for 17.1 percent of the total land area of the nation[33].

Nepal, which is perched on the southern slopes of the Himalayan Alps, is as ethnically varied as the landscape it inhabits. Historically, the Nepalese are descended from three great migrations in India, Tibet, and central Asia[34]. The Newars of the Kathmandu valley and the aboriginal Tharus of the southern Terai area were among the first settlers in the region, which dates back thousands of years. However, over 100 regional and indigenous languages are spoken across the nation[35]. Nepali, the country's official language, is derived from Sanskrit and is close to Hindi, and it is spoken by around 90 percent of the country's people (although often as a second or third language)[36]. The languages of Hindi and English are also spoken by many Nepalese in government and business.

Nepal's First Five-Year Plan, implemented in 1956, was the first instance of planned economic growth in the country, with a mixed economic strategy serving as the state's guiding concept[37]. Nepal liberalized its economy in recent years by implementing a broad variety of economic reforms[38]. In major sectors of the economy such as manufacturing, commerce, foreign investment, financial services, and international business transactions, the effects of these changes have been spectacular. The reform and restructuring process that has been underway has played a critical role in making the economy more investment- friendly, transparent, market-oriented, and efficient. The implementation of structural changes has laid a solid foundation for future economic growth and development.

33 Geography of Nepal | Physical Features of Nepal | Nepal Travel.
   https://www.nepalvisitors.com/ geography-of-nepal/
34 https://basecampadventure.com/people-of-nepal/
35 https://www.devkumarsunuwar.com.np/nepal-s-indigenous-languages-on-the-verge-of-extinction
36 https://wordinvent.com/a-brief-history-of-nepali-language/
37 https://www.npc.gov.np/images/category/fifth_eng.pdf
38 https://www.nrb.org.np/contents/uploads/2021/09/vol19_art3.pdf

The establishment of joint venture banks and private financial institutions, privatization of state-owned enterprises, and an expansion of the role of the private sector in the economy have all been supported as a result of this policy. Incentives for private sector engagement in economic activities have been supported by market-oriented economic policies, which have reduced the role of the government to that of a facilitator and provider of conditions to help the private sector become more efficient and competitive. In a similar vein, the elimination of licensing requirements and quantitative restrictions in industry and trade, the simplification of regulatory processes, the provision of current account convertibility, the expansion of the areas of foreign direct investment, and a slew of other reform measures have created an environment conducive to increasing efficiency and competition in a wide range of economic activities.

According to the World Bank, Nepal is one of the world's poorest nations, with a per capita income of around US $427[39]. According to national calorie-to-GNP ratios, an estimated 55 percent of the population lives below the poverty level of $1.25 per day[40]. Since its inception in the mid-20th century, Nepal has been an isolated and rural civilization. It joined the modern age in 1951 without having built schools or hospitals, constructed roads, installed electric power, or established any industry or public service. Since the 1950s, however, the government has made significant strides toward achieving sustainable economic development, and it is dedicated to a policy of economic reform.

It is predicted that the actual Gross Domestic Product (GDP) would expand by just 3.5 percent in the fiscal year 2015, compared to the planned 5.5 percent growth[41]. Nepal is still in the early stages of industrial growth, with the industrial sector accounting for around 15 percent of the country's total economic output. The manufacturing industry contributes around 9% of the country's gross domestic product (GDP). According to

---

39 https://www.worldbank.org/en/country/nepal/overview
40 https://documents1.worldbank.org/curated/en/190711468749798158/pdf/multi0page.pd
  f
41 https://www.worldbank.org/en/country/nepal/publication/nepaldevelopmentupdate

the latest available data, as of July 16, 2021, there were 8454 industries of all sizes registered with the Department of Industries (DoI)[42]. Agriculture continues to be Nepal's most important economic sector, providing employment for more than 75 percent of the population and contributing to 33 percent of the country's GDP. Only roughly 25% of the overall land area is cultivable, with the remaining 33% consisting of forest and the rest being hilly. Rice and wheat are the primary food crops in Nepal. The lowland Terai region creates an agricultural surplus, which is used to supply food to the food-stressed hill communities. Because Nepal relies on agriculture, the amount of rain received during the yearly monsoon season significantly impacts economic development.

1.3 Geography of Nepal

Nepal is a landlocked nation in South Asia[43], bordered by China to the north and India to the east, south and west[44], The nation has a total land area of 147,516 square kilometers and is located between the latitudes of 28°N and 84°E[45]. Nepal is located in the temperate zone, north of the Tropic of Cancer, and has a tropical climate. The whole distance from east to west is around 800 kilometers, although north to south is just 150 to 250 kilometers. Nepal is home to extensive water systems that drain south into India[46]. In terms of geography, the nation may be split into three major geographical regions: the Himalayan Region, the Mid-Hill Region, and the Terai Region. While Mt. Everest (8,848 m) is the highest point in the nation, the lowest point is in the Terai plains of Kechana Kalan in Jhapa, which is the most southern point (60 m). The Terai area has a width ranging from 26 km to 32 km and an elevation varying from 60 m to 305

---

42 https://doind.gov.np/

43 https://www.researchgate.net/figure/1-Nepal-a-landlocked-country-in-South-Asia_ fig1_306909815

44 Sagarmatha Zone - Wikipedia. https://en.wikipedia.org/wiki/Sagarmatha_Zone

45 https://myrepublica.nagariknetwork.com/news/nepal-s-new-map-covers-an-area-of-147-516- sq-km-10-000-copies-being-printed/

46 https://dras.in/politics-of-water-between-india-and-nepal/

m[47]. The Terai region has a breadth ranging from 26 km to 32 km and an elevation ranging from 60 m to 305 m. It accounts for around 17 percent of the country's overall land area. In the north, the Siwalik zone (3,000 to 4,000 feet) and the Mahabharat range (1,525 to 4,877m) give way to the Duns (valleys), which include the Sindhu valleys, Chitwan and Dang.

North of the Mahabharat range, in the Midlands (600–3,500 m), are the two lovely valleys of Kathmandu and Pokhara, which the Himalayas separates[48]. The mountainous terrain starts at 3000 meters above sea level[49]. It ascends to alpine meadows and temperate woods, restricted by the tree line at 4,000 meters above sea level and the snow line at 5000 meters above sea level. Nepal is home to eight of the world's[50] tallest peaks (out of fourteen) that rise over 8000 meters: Mt. Everest, Mt. Kailash, Mt. Makalu, Mt. Kailash II, Mt. Makalu II, Mount Everest (8,848 meters), Kanchenjunga (8,586 meters), Lhotse (8,516 meters), Makalu (8,485 meters), Cho Oyu (8,188 meters), Dhaulagiri (8,167 meters), Manaslu (8,163 meters), and Annapurna (8,091 meters) are the highest mountains in the world[51]. Mountains in the inner Himalayan valley (above 3,600 meters altitude), such as Mustang and Dolpo, are cold deserts with topographical features similar to those of the Tibetan plateau. Home to the "water towers of South Asia," Nepal has over 6,000 rivers that are either snow-fed or reliant on precipitation.

The Mahakali, Karnali, Narayani and Koshi rivers, which originate in the Himalayas, are among the perennial rivers in the world. The Midlands and the Mahabharat range sources medium-sized rivers like the West Rapti, Bagmati and Mechi. Of the 163 wetlands that have been documented, the nine Ramsar Sites that have been internationally

47 https://www.shepherdholidays.com/blog/geography-of-nepal
48 https://bd.nepalembassy.gov.np/blog/geography/
49 10 Best Mountains In Nepal That Will Take Your Breath Away. https://www.xvell.com/10-best- mountains-in-nepal/
50 Where is Nepal Located on Map, Nepal Map in Asia and World - Tibet Travel. https://www. tibettravel.org/nepal-map/nepal-location.html
51 https://boundlessadventure.com/blog/top-14-over-8000-meters-highest-mountains-in-the- world/

recognized are Beeshazari and Associated Lakes, Jagadishpur Reservoir, Ghodaghodi Lake Area, Gosaikunda and Associated Lakes, Phoksundo Lakes), Rara Lake and Mai Pokhari. There are more than 30 natural caverns in the nation, but only a handful of them are accessible by road, making them a popular tourist attraction. Maratika Cave (also known as Alesha) is a Buddhist and Hindu pilgrimage site located in the Himalayan Mountains. Siddha Cave is located below Bandipur, near Bimal Nagar, on the Kathmandu-Pokhara route, below the town of Bandipur. Besides caves, Pokhara is home to several other natural wonders, including the Bats' shed (Mahendra Gufa) or Mahendra Cave[52]. Lure and Tashia Kibum caverns in Mustang, which have old paintings and chortens going back to the 13th century and are among the several caves around Lo Manthang.

1.4 Climate of Nepal

The summers in the north of Nepal are cool, and the winters are harsh. However, in the south, it is quite hot but becomes chilly during the cold months. Nepal has five distinct seasons, which are as follows: spring, summer, monsoon, autumn, and winter[53]. Summer temperatures in the Tara (southern Nepal) may reach 40° C and even 45° C in certain regions, while winter temperatures can vary from 7° C to 23° C in some areas. Summers in mountainous areas, hills, and valleys are mild. However, winter temperatures may fall to below zero in the mountains and valleys. The Kathmandu Valley has a nice environment, with average summer temperatures ranging from 20°C to 35°C and typical winter temperatures ranging from 2°C to 12°C[54]. The average temperature in Nepal drops by 6 degrees Celsius for every 1,000 meters of elevation gained[55]. It serves as a barrier against the chilly winds coming in from Central Asia throughout the winter, and it also serves as the northern limit for the monsoon rains. Some areas, such as Manang and Mustang, are typically dry because they

52 https://www.landnepal.com/details/2133.html
53 https://www.vivaanadventure.com/seasons-in-nepal/
54 https://weatherspark.com/y/111107/Average-Weather-in-Kathmandu-Nepal-Year-Round
55 https://www.yetitrailadventure.com/nepal/climate-in-nepal.html

are in the rain-shadow cast by the mountains behind them. During the monsoon season (June-September), Nepal receives 80 percent of its total annual rainfall. Winter rains are more noticeable in the western hills than in the eastern hills. The average annual rainfall is 1,600 mm. However, it varies according to the eco-climatic zone, with 3,345 mm in Pokhara and less than 300 mm in Mustang.

There are no restrictions on traveling to and through Nepal based on the season. Even in December and January, when winter is at its harshest, there is enough dazzling sunshine and breathtaking scenery to make up for it. Similar to most trekking destinations in Nepal, the ideal times are during the spring and fall seasons. Rhododendrons blossom in the spring, and the clearest sky may be seen following the monsoon season in October and November when the temperature cools. Nepal can be visited throughout the year. Maritime and continental influences impact Nepal's climate, which is distinguished by four different seasons. Spring, which lasts from March through May, is warm and humid, with rain showers and temperatures about 22 degrees Celsius. The monsoon season, which lasts from June through August, is when the hills grow lush and green with rain. During heat waves, temperatures may reach up to 30 degrees Celsius and even more. Trekking in much of Nepal is tough and unpleasant at this time of year since the routes are muddy and rutted. The autumn season, which runs from September to November, is cold and clear, making it the most popular time to go trekking.

Temperatures are not too warm, with daytime maximums of approximately 25°C and cold evenings a minimum of 10°C. It seldom rains for more than one or two days over the fall and winter seasons, and the weather is generally pleasant. During the winter months of December to February, it is very chilly at night, with temperatures sometimes dropping below zero[56]. The maximum temperatures, on the other hand, may still reach up to 20°C. The mountains, including some of the highest

---

56 https://www.climatestotravel.com/climate/nepal

peaks, are then blanketed with snow. Clothing should be chosen according to the location and time of day; nonetheless, it is advisable to have light and warm clothing on hand since the nights may be rather chilly in the summer. Generally speaking, warm clothing is required in mountainous terrain.

Chitwan National Park has an average temperature of 10 to 15 degrees warmer than Kathmandu, and temperatures in the middle of the day may reach far beyond 80 degrees Fahrenheit (32 degrees Celsius)[57]. Despite this, it is necessary to dress in layers for wildlife drives in the early cold hours, when average temperatures are normally between 40°F and 50°F. Nepal has the occasional rain shower throughout February through April, with rainfall quantities less than 1 inch on average. However, although most of Nepal's mountainous regions are located on the southern side of the Tibetan Plateau, a few spots are located on the opposite side of the mountain range. Several smaller and lesser-known regions of Nepal, including Dolpa, Manang and a few other smaller and lesser-known areas, are located in the rain shadow of the Himalaya, which means that the mountains block the monsoon rains that sweep up from India between June and September.

This region of Nepal is significantly drier than the rest of Nepal, and as a result, the terrain is extremely distinct. The accessibility of the region is also different from the rest of Nepal. Between June and September, most hiking regions are too wet to be used for trekking; nevertheless, these are the finest months to visit sites in the rain shadow since they are dry during this time. Getting there, on the other hand, might still be a challenge. Mustang, for example, can only be reached through a short flight across the mountains (or a lengthy and miserable bus journey), which is often postponed during the monsoon season due to the rain. As a result of their greater altitude, areas in the rain shadow have frigid winters and milder and drier weather throughout the rest of the year. As temperatures reach

---

57 https://www.nathab.com/know-before-you-go/asia-the-pacific/bhutan-nepal/weather-climate/

an unbearable level in late May and early June, Nepalese look forward to the coming of the monsoon, which washes up the continent from India and brings relief. The rainy season in Kathmandu typically begins in mid- June and lasts until the end of September. It does not rain continuously throughout the day during the monsoon season, although the sky is often overcast, and the streets are often muddy. Temperatures are slightly lower than they were during the suffocating pre-monsoon weeks, but humidity is quite high.

Nepal's hilly and mountainous regions are free of malaria-carrying insects. However, dengue outbreaks in Kathmandu during the monsoon season in previous years indicate that using an effective insect repellent is essential if you must go to Nepal during the monsoon season[58]. Shivaratri and Holi, two Hindu holidays celebrated in Nepal[59], mark the arrival of spring, and both are celebrated in the first week of March. Even though temperatures vary around the nation, in the capital, the average daily temperature in early March is a moderate 68 degrees, increasing to a less comfortable 86 degrees by late May. Temperatures are becoming hotter sooner in the Terai and later in the Himalayas, but the overall trend of rising high temperatures throughout March, April, and May continues to hold.

1.5 Ten Facts about Poverty in Nepal

According to Amelia Merchant article[60], 25 percent of people live below the poverty line, on 50 cents per day. Nepal is now among the world's poorest nations as a result. There are significant rates of sickness, hunger, and infant mortality. Fortunately, Nepal's economy has barely budged during the previous several years. Here are 10 facts about poverty in Nepal:
- The country's living standards have been significantly impacted by

---

58 http://mybheja.blogspot.com/2022/09/dengue-spreads-in-cities.html
59 https://www.missionsummittreks.com/maha-shiva-ratri-and-holi-in-nepal/
60 https://borgenproject.org/ten-facts-about-poverty-in-nepal/

displacement. Relief Web states that between 1996 and 2006, hundreds of people died, and many more were displaced as a result of the civil conflict between the Maoists and the Nepali government's military forces.

- In Nepal, there are about 5 million undernourished individuals. High food prices and restricted access to farming in rural regions are two factors contributing to this. Hunger is caused by the high cost of food, which is expensive for those living in poverty.

- Nepal has experienced several natural catastrophes. Earthquakes in Nepal add to the nation's instability because of its weak political stability and suffering economy. People are compelled to discover new sources of income after losing their houses and employment. Following a natural disaster, women are frequently more at risk of being victims of trafficking.

- The crooked nature of Nepal's administration is well recognized. The nation came in third place among corrupt nations in South Asia. Abuse of authority leads to a skewed economic structure and unfair distribution of resources, exacerbating the issue of poverty in Nepal.

- Nepal has significant child mortality rates, which are a result of poverty. In Nepal, 35 infants per 1,000 births died before turning five in 2016. This can be ascribed to the fact that Nepal has a large number of underdeveloped areas without access to health care or education.

- Nepal's geography has an impact on its capacity to reduce poverty. Nepal is a landlocked, mountainous region, which makes resource transportation and development challenges.

- It is challenging to achieve headway against poverty in Nepal due to a lack of modern farming techniques. Over 85 percent of the population in Nepal relies on agriculture as the major method of survival. However, sluggish farming practices remain a problem. Additionally, farmers have not received sufficient infrastructure from the Nepali government.

- Unemployment and underemployment greatly contribute to poverty rates in Nepal. The unemployment rate was 3.4 percent in 2016. One of the main causes of poverty is a lack of well-paying jobs.
- The Nepalese poor find it difficult to own a home due to rising housing costs. Up to 10% of city dwellers live in squats. The rate of rural-urban movement has also increased dramatically in recent years, driving up the cost of housing in cities even more.
- There are several non-profit organizations, such as Habitat for Humanity, that are trying to aid the people of Nepal. The housing shortage in Nepal has received particular attention from Habitat for Humanity. Together, they are constructing 2.3 houses each hour with their partners. Communities in Nepal may be empowered and improve their quality of life thanks to groups like these.

1.5 Making a Success of Nepal

Because of Nepal's new federal government, decisions on public services and economic growth are being made closer to the people. A better fit between service delivery and local objectives is an opportunity to enhance services in this area. However, the country needs clearly defined indicators of achievement and comprehensive and trustworthy data so that local, state, and federal governments can monitor development progress, learn what is working, and make course adjustments as necessary. Strong data systems must be put in place as soon as possible, and immediate action must be taken.

The Sustainable Development Goals (SDGs) might serve as a framework to help achieve this goal. Political scientist Alexis de Tocqueville observed that historically, a federal system "brings together the many advantages of great and small size countries." Because subnational governments are physically closer to the people who elected them, they may establish policies and services more responsive to local concerns. Furthermore, since governments are closer to their residents, the constituents are better positioned to evaluate their performance – and, in certain cases, to determine whether or not to vote for them again in the future. Nepal is making strides toward the establishment of a federal form of government.

You can see exciting examples of local innovation while traveling around Nepal, including investments in specialist services to address local health issues, targeted efforts to increase access to educational opportunities for girls from the most vulnerable communities, and thoughtful planning to build resilience against environmental hazards[61]. However, to make sound decisions on policies and investments, it is necessary to access high-quality data at the local and state levels. It is more probable that subnational governments will get the most value out of every rupee of taxpayers' money if they can base their choices on reliable data on the costs per unit of decreasing maternal mortality or creating economic possibilities. Even the most dedicated state or local leaders will be operating with a considerable disadvantage if they do not access reliable data. Voters will also have a more difficult time determining whether or not politicians have been delivering on their promises. Nepal is a varied nation, and there is a great deal of variance in the issues that local governments encounter and their performance.

Over the next few months and years, there will be significant work to be done to clarify precisely which functions should be delivered by which sphere of government to ensure that local and state governments have the capable staff and effective systems required to deliver, to foster effective coordination between different governments, and to match financial resources with responsibilities. The government has tasked the World Bank and the United Nations Development Program (UNDP) with conducting a federal needs assessment to map out some of the most

---

61   Making a Success of Federalism: Putting Data at the Heart of Nepal's
     https://www.undp.org/ nepal/news/making-success-federalism-putting-data-heart-
     nepal%E2%80%99s-decision- making

pressing issues[62]. However, in the end, Nepal will have to discover its answers – and in doing so, it will be able to establish a kind of federalism that is beneficial to the country. Once again, very accurate real-time data may be critical in this situation. With reliable statistics on progress toward development objectives, it will be simpler for policymakers to determine which governments are doing well, accelerate lesson learning across governments, and to guarantee that those who are failing get more assistance. A common framework of indicators throughout the nation would be vital in assisting Nepal in tracking progress toward its development targets. The Sustainable Development Goals (SDGs), adopted by the United Nations General Assembly in 2015[63], might serve as an overarching delivery framework[64].

A worldwide effort has resulted in the development of 169 objectives and a comprehensive set of indicators to aid in measuring progress toward the achievement of the 17 Sustainable Development Goals. The globally agreed-upon Sustainable Development Goals (SDGs) were comprehensive, spanning a wide range of development goals ranging from basic health care to justice and from economic development to climate resilience. Consequently, they might potentially offer an ideal framework for Nepal to utilize to monitor achievement at the municipal, state, and federal levels if they are carefully prioritized. Most notably, Nepal has already begun regionalizing the Sustainable Development Goals (SDGs) across the nation. Given the critical role that data plays in the effective implementation of the federal system, Nepal must invest rapidly in robust federalism-ready data management systems as soon as possible. To establish confidence and legitimacy in the National Statistical System, the Central Bureau of Statistics (CBS) will play an important role in this process.

---

62 https://www.undp.org/nepal/news/making-success-federalism-
    putting-da- ta-heart-nepal%E2%80%99s-decision-making
63 Agenda 2030 us map - bapb.thegenie.shop.
    https://bapb.thegenie.shop/en/agenda-2030- us-map.html
64 https://sdgs.un.org/goals

For the CBS to generate reliable, unbiased data that all of Nepal's 761 governments can use to inform decision-making, the federal, provincial, and local governments must place their faith in it. Nepal cannot afford to squander time and money on the duplication of data collecting by multiple levels of government or on arguments between administrations over statistical issues that has happened in the past. Continuing to connect with local and state governments to understand their data requirements, interests, and capabilities will be critical for CBS in the coming years.   The next census will provide an especially valuable chance to better understand development requirements throughout the whole country of Nepal[65]. Beginning early and building on extensive conversations with subnational governments around the country, consultations on the census will be critical to ensuring a successful outcome.

The CBS must begin this job immediately, and it must get support from all sides of the political spectrum. A well-planned and inclusive census would yield data that will aid in sound decision-making and expedite Nepal's development; yet a badly designed census runs the risk of causing misunderstanding and confusion among the general public.

---

65 https://blogs.worldbank.org/governance/how-data-can-benefit-nepal

Chapter 2: Physical Infrastructure & Trade of Nepal

With the arrival of the private sector into the telecommunications business, the industry has progressed reasonably. Over a nationwide network, the operators offer fixed-line and mobile cellular services, including 3G services. The providers also provide Internet access. On 15th December 2020, the National Telecommunications Authority announced figures showing 841,698 users of fixed-line telephones and 9.195 million customers to cellular mobile services[66]. In addition to this, the nation has an estimated 1.902 million data/internet subscribers. With 37.95 percent penetration in telephony services subscribership (fixed-line and mobile cellular telephone service) and 6.78 percent penetration in data/Internet services, investors have a considerable opportunity to reach out to the remaining population. Nepal has a population of 28,951,852 people (estimated for July 2021), with a population growth rate of 1.419 percent[67]. The population between the ages of 15 and 64- accounts for 59.2 percent of the total population, with 8,094,494 males and 8,812,675 females making up the total.

The population between the ages of 0- and 14-years forms 36.6 percent of the total population, with the remainder being above 64 years. According to 2020 estimates, urbanization is growing at 4.9 percent per

---

66 https://www.nta.gov.np/en/
67 https://www.worldometers.info/world-population/nepal-population/

year, with urban regions accounting for 17 percent of the total population in 2020. The average life expectancy for the whole population is 65.81 years old. Nepal has a literacy rate of 48 percent, with 62.7 percent of the male population being literate and 34.9 percent of the female population being literate. According to some estimates, the spending on education accounts for 3.8 percent of the country's gross domestic product. According to some earlier estimates, the unemployment rate in Nepal is 46 percent, while the population living below the poverty level is 24.7 percent.

2.1 Air Services, Railways & Telecommunication

Nepal has 54 airports[68]. These include three international airports, regional hub airports (Nepalgunj, Bhairahawa, and Dhangadhi), 43 other domestic airports, and five airports that are currently under development (Hirahara, Pokhara, and Dhangadhi) (Kalikow, Kamal Bazar, Mainchain, Shilshole, and Samachar). Air services are provided by 34 airports out of the total number of airports. Nepal has signed Bilateral Air Service Agreements (ASA) with 35 nations, including India, as part of its international expansion. Kathmandu is linked to major cities like New Delhi, Mumbai, Kolkata, Varanasi, and Lucknow. In addition, Kathmandu is linked to Dhaka, Karachi, Bangkok, Singapore, Shanghai, Doha, Abu Dhabi, and Muscat by a network of international flights.

There are efforts underway to expand railway services inside Nepal and India. Currently, Nepal has just 59-kilometers of narrow-gauge railway, but this is expected to rise shortly. When India and Nepal signed a rail service agreement in May 2020, the agreement provided the expansion of freight train service to Nepal's inland container depot (ICD). Beginning on July 16, 2020, the ICD was in full function.

2.2 Trade

As a result of the above, Nepal's commerce with other nations is

---

68 https://nepalinerd.com/domestic-international-airports-in-nepal/

growing as well. The full convertibility of the Nepalese currency in the current account, the provision for maintaining a foreign exchange account for earnings from exports, the implementation of a time-bound duty refund scheme on exports, and the de-licensing of imports are all important factors in Nepal's efforts to diversify its foreign trade. Imports have increased rapidly in recent years, rising from US$1.6 billion (26 percent of GDP) in the fiscal year 2020-01 to US$5.2 billion (30 percent of GDP) in the fiscal year 2020-10, partly as a result of booming spending made possible by remittances from abroad. Exports have stayed below $1 billion in value and have steadily decreased from 13 percent to 7 percent over the last decade as a percentage of GDP.

The country's exports of readymade clothes, carpets, and Pashmina, formerly the country's principal exports, have dropped[69]. Official remittances increased from around 13.8 percent of GDP to approximately 22 percent of GDP in the fiscal year 2020-09. Because it does not consider inflows from India and informal routes, it is less than the overall quantity of money. Monetary growth has been strong in recent years, fueled by a large inflow of remittances from abroad. Nepal's imports and exports are heavily influenced by Indian trade policy. The Commerce Treaty between India and Nepal is anticipated to expand Nepalese trade to unprecedented heights. In the case of bilateral transactions, the use of other foreign currencies with US dollar equivalent status has relieved the bilateral commerce of DRP complications. India accounts for 58 percent of Nepal's goods trade and one-third of the country's trade in services, and it is therefore the country's most important trading partner[70].

2.3 Import & Export

Nepalese imports have grown exponentially in recent years, and the country's economy has experienced significant structural changes. Among

---

69 https://kathmandupost.com/money/2017/05/28/pashmina-exports-down-68- percent-due-to- lower-demand-in-europe

70 https://www.indembkathmandu.gov.in/page/about-trade-and-commerce/

the most important products imported are capital goods, industrial raw materials, and consumer goods. Total imports increased by 43.9 percent from the middle of July 2020 to the middle of March 2021, reaching NRs 253.74 billion, compared to a 26.3 percent increase the same time the previous year. The percentage of Indian imports in overall imports decreased significantly from 56.3 percent to 54.2 percent this year. In comparison, the share of other nations increased from 43.7 percent to 45.8 percent during this time. Compared to the previous fiscal year, import growth increased by 45.4 percent this year. This compares to a 6.6 percent increase in the previous fiscal year. During the period from mid-March 2020 to mid-March 2021, imports from India increased by 38.5 percent, reaching NRs 137.41 billion (US$ 1.3 billion) (NRs 116.33 billion from countries other than India). When comparing the same time of the previous year, imports had had a typical growth rate of 12.1%.

During the period under consideration, the total value of products imported from India via payments in convertible foreign currency reached NRs 18.26 billion, representing a 40 percent increase over the previous year. Imports of raw and manufactured goods from India remained at 36.9 percent and 63.1 percent, respectively, in the period under consideration. In contrast, they were at 42.2 percent and 57.8 percent respectively, in the same period the previous year. Total exports increased by 16.2 percent during the first eight months of 2020-09 but declined by 8 percent in the same fiscal year 2020-10, totaling NRs 40.41 billion. Despite a nominal rise in exports to India (by 3.4 percent) from 60.9 percent to 64.3 percent during the review period, overall exports (to both India and other countries) did not expand much during the time under review. In the review period of the previous fiscal year, the ratio of exports to imports was 24.9 percent.

In the equivalent period of the current fiscal year, the ratio fell to 15.9 percent due to a major increase in imports and a considerable decline in exports. Compared to the previous year, overall export decreased by 7.1

percent in US Dollar terms, compared to a 1.9 percent loss in the previous year. This decrease in export earnings (measured in US dollars) is also attributable to the 7.8 percent increase in the value of the Nepalese rupee relative to the US dollar from the middle of July 2020 and the middle of March 2021. Exports to India, which had climbed by 3.7 percent during the first eight months of the previous fiscal year, shrank to NRs 25.96 billion during the same time this year, representing a 2.9 percent reduction from the same period the previous year.

Over this period, exports of items such as polyester yarn, jute bags, and jute cutting, textiles (including SS pipe), herbs (including Chalandra's), Hamala (including Pashmina), and copper wire rods have increased, while exports of vegetable ghee, lentils, flour, yarn, toothpaste, and noodles have decreased[71]. The group-wise structure of commodity exports to India reveals that the proportion of primary and manufactured goods in the first eight months of the previous fiscal year was 30.0 percent and 70.0 percent, respectively, while the proportions are 27.5 percent and 72.5 percent in the same period of this fiscal year.

During the first eight months of 2020-10, exports suffered a considerable decline, while imports increased dramatically. In addition, the overall trade imbalance increased by almost double to 61.2 percent of GDP, or NRs 213.33 billion, due to a larger base of imported goods. Exports to India increased by 53.8 percent during the time under review, while exports to other countries increased by 70.1 percent during the same period. The trade imbalance with India increased by 53.8 percent during the period under review. During the same time the previous year, the deficit with India climbed by 15.6 percent, while the deficit with other nations increased by 53.4 percent. As a result of a widening trade imbalance, Nepal had a balance of payments (Bop) deficit of US$ 36 million for the first time in its history from 2020 to 2021.

As a result of the negative balance of payments and the consequent

---

71 https://in.nepalembassy.gov.np/trade-and-commerce/

drop in the level of foreign currency reserve, the situation has deteriorated, with the balance of payments now in deficit and the level of foreign exchange reserve declining. It is estimated that the entire foreign currency reserves of the banking sector have decreased by 15.6% between July 2020 and March 2021, amounting to NRs 236.34 billion, as opposed to an increase of 27.4% during the same time the previous year.

While foreign liabilities increased by 30.9 percent during the same time last year, they declined by 7.5 percent to NRs 55.01 billion during the same period this year, compared to a substantial increase of 30.9 percent during the same period the year before. As a result, net foreign assets, which had grown by 27.4 percent in the first eight months of the previous fiscal year, have declined by 15.1 percent to NRs 187.67 billion, a reduction of 15.1 percent from the previous fiscal year.

The industry is unquestionably the cornerstone of long-term economic growth and the building of a self-sufficient economy. In recognition of this reality, the new amended Industrial Policy has been developed and implemented. Its objectives include fostering an industry-friendly and conducive investment environment for both domestic and international investors, increasing industrial production and productivity, increasing employment opportunities, and facilitating import replacement and export promotion, among other things.

2.4 Nepal-China Relations

The first religious contacts between Nepal and China date back to the early fifth century when monks and academics often visited. On the reciprocal ideals of the Five Principles of Peaceful Coexistence— friendship, understanding, mutual support, collaboration, and respect for each other's sensibilities—official diplomatic relations were established in 1955. On August 1st, 1955, diplomatic relations were established between the two nations, thereby solidifying their ties. Since the two countries' economic links were established in 1956, China has given Nepal grants, loans with low-interest rates, and concessional loans. The first such deal, titled "Agreement between China and Nepal on Economic Aid," was signed in 1956 and included a variety of topics, including infrastructure development, hydropower projects, healthcare, and education[72]. Beijing unveiled the BRI framework in 2013, but it took Nepal almost five years to formally join the initiative. Shanker Das Bairagi, the foreign minister of Nepal, and Yu Hong, the Chinese ambassador there, signed a Memorandum of Understanding (MoU) on the Belt and Road Initiative (BRI) between Nepal and China in 2017.

The course of Nepal's foreign policy is determined by its physical closeness to China and India. Rama Kant argues that economics and cultural similarity are insufficiently important for Nepal-China cooperation. There is a tiny market for Chinese goods in Nepal, but there is no sizable Chinese community to influence choices. In Nepal, internal politics had a significant impact on the relationship between China and India. The Nepali monarchy, which received internal backing from some communist elements, was valued by the Chinese. However, the Nepali Congress was a party supported by India that was anti-communist. Since the 2008 collapse of the monarchy, Nepal has been governed by a federal three-tier system with a non-aligned foreign policy ingrained in the guiding principles and state policy of the Constitution.

OBOR (BRI) projects in Nepal

Nepal must turn elsewhere for transportation connections since it is a landlocked nation without access to the sea, which makes it difficult for it to conduct trade and commerce for economic growth. Nepal will benefit greatly from OBOR in terms of trade, business, tourism, and commerce. The BRI framework is seen as a helpful growth accelerator in Nepal. China has spent in building roads and railroads. Energy, tourism, a free trade zone, and irrigation are among the investment options, with

72 https://www.oboreurope.com/en/obor-in-nepal/

35 projects managed by a Commercial Counselor Office in Kathmandu. China and Nepal are separated by a 1,415 kilometers border. There are 18 border crossing points that serve as important trade routes between China and Nepal. The most significant of these are Kerrang (Ky-irong) and Kuti (Nyi-Lan). The border crossing locations at Wollangchung, Khumbu, Tukuche, and Karnali are also significant. The Rasuwa Gadhi- Kerong border crossing is both the most significant and challenging road access between Nepal and China. As one of the most popular tourist sites, Rasuwa, where the Langtang National Park is located, would benefit greatly from the development of road and rail infrastructure.

Chapter 3: Entrepreneurship in Nepal: Challenges and Opportunities

Many individuals in Nepalese society are entrepreneurs because they have the necessary knowledge, aptitude, and skills to take advantage of opportunities for economic gain. Entrepreneurship is a kind of commercial activity that business owners practice and it is defined as the act of creating an ornament by a goldsmith. Entrepreneurship is the process of establishing new businesses. It entails imagination and inventiveness. The whole concept of entrepreneurship revolves around self-employment, which in turn creates job prospects for others. Bridging the gap between science and marketplace, entrepreneurialism starts new firms, and provides innovative goods and services.

Entrepreneurship, according to Peter Drucker (1970)[73] and K. Knight (1967) is about taking risks. It is the process of creating new values that did not previously exist; it is the practice of starting new organizations, particularly new businesses[74]; and it involves the creation of new wealth through the implementation of new concepts, among other things. According to Robert (1985), entrepreneurship is defined as the process of producing something valuable by dedicating the required time and effort, taking on social risk, and then reaping the advantages of monetary

---

73 Drucker, P. (1970). The new markets and the new capitalism. The Public Interest, 21, 44.
74 Entrepreneurship - Business Research Launch Pad.
   https://www.d.umn.edu/~jvileta/entrepre- neurship.html

and personal happiness as a result. Nepal has not been unaffected by the worldwide trend of entrepreneurship, which is gaining momentum in countries all over the globe. However, the internal climate of the nation does not seem to be sufficiently encouraging to allow the entrepreneurial spirit to blossom to its full potential. As a result, we are attempting to determine what the possibilities are and what the constraints are to entrepreneurship in Nepal. Entrepreneurship entails more than just starting up new businesses. It is about finding new and better ways to solve issues and provide value to the world. Entrepreneurs must take chances on innovative concepts that have not yet been proven and confirmed in the market to succeed in business. Although entrepreneurs face a significant risk of failing due to their inventive nature, there is a great likelihood that the goods and services they develop will be disruptive enough to create a whole new market and set of opportunities.

3.1 Why is Entrepreneurship Important in Nepal?

Approximately 10,689,842 people in Nepal are under the age of 30, according to the 2021 Census (40.3 percent)[75]. Nepal is poised to flourish because it is youthful, active, and eager to engage in the global economy. It is also a democracy. There are several investment options available in this area. A critical role in the long-term economic growth of the country is played by entrepreneurship. Nepal's future cannot be predicated only   on international assistance and remittances, as has been suggested. If we want to continue ahead on the path of sustainable economic development, we must provide sufficient support and create an atmosphere conducive to new entrepreneurship and innovation. Entrepreneurship is vital because it will produce jobs, but it will also have a significant influence on the lives of young people in general. Nepal's youthful and enthusiastic populace is leaving the country daily in pursuit of new possibilities. If all of Nepal's residents are involved in entrepreneurship, the country's need for foreign

---

75 Abstract - Social Change. https://socialchange.org.np/wp-content/uploads/2022/07/ YOUTHS-PARTICIPATION-IN-THE-GOVERNANCE-PROCESS-IN-Nepal.pdf

aid would be reduced significantly.

Several investment options are available in this area. Investing in and encouraging entrepreneurship is one of the most significant ways to accelerate the country's economic development while remaining competitive in a rapidly changing global environment. Nepal's future cannot be solely reliant on international help and remittances shortly. If we want to continue ahead on the path of sustainable economic development, we must provide sufficient support and create an atmosphere conducive to new entrepreneurship and innovation. Entrepreneurship is vital because it will produce jobs, but it will also have a significant influence on the lives of young people in general. Nepal's youthful and enthusiastic populace are leaving the country daily in pursuit of new possibilities. Entrepreneurship must grow sustainably in Nepal to provide optimism, dignity, self-esteem, and a good culture that encourages people to remain and contribute to the country's development.

3.2 What Are the Challenges for Entrepreneurship in Nepal?

There are several opportunities for entrepreneurial growth in Nepal; yet there are significant obstacles to the entrance and smooth operations for those who want to start a business. For our nations, the most significant issues are a lack of access to technology and infrastructure. The primary difficulty of entrepreneurship in Nepal is the scarcity of highly qualified experts in the field of new technology relevant to our commercial operations and the inability to make the necessary adjustments. In the context of Nepal, the vast majority of banks and financial institutions only give financial assistance to students who have degrees from overseas institutions. When young people accomplish anything in our country, there may be issues with collateral and other aspects of their actions.

Youths with fantastic ideas cannot launch their ventures due to a lack of funding, which is a significant obstacle to the creation of new businesses. Nepalese culture is traditional because most individuals prefer to spend their money on land, gold and silver savings, building structures, and consuming luxury products rather than investing in new ventures or starting their businesses. Parents are often unsupportive of startups and are wary about taking a chance on their children. High-profile jobs and government positions are associated with our society's mentality. As a result, our societal judgments are also a source of difficulty for businesses. The process of registering a corporation, complying with rules, and paying taxes is complicated and time-consuming. In other circumstances, if the company concept is something new and original, there may be no legal need to register the firm at all. The prospect of taxation is always a demotivating element for new businesses as well as established enterprises. Customs duties are very hefty when bringing new technology and other electrical materials into the country. Startups may contribute to the development of a country in a short period if the legislation and policies are favorable to new businesses and entrepreneurs.

Corruption is the most pervasive and pernicious source of evil in public institutions. People's distrust of public organizations is so profound that they have little faith in their ability to collaborate with them and achieve sustainable development objectives. Corruption is one of the most serious issues facing the public sector all over the globe. Nepal does not have effective intellectual property protection legislation in place. As a result, the majority of breakthrough company ideas are stolen and used by others. For business growth in Nepal, it is necessary to have strong intellectual property rights protection and legislation in place. More hidden barriers for entrepreneurship exist in addition to these, such as a lack of training and development, a lack of governmental action, and the absence of a practical education system. Despite the tremendous promise and pressing need for entrepreneurship growth in Nepal, there are several obstacles to the entrance and successful operations in the business world in the country. If a young person wants to study or go abroad, banks, financial institutions, and parents will give them a large sum of money, but none will risk investing in a business. Because of a shortage of funding, many young people with excellent ideas cannot get their businesses off the ground. There is no availability of business loans at all without using the real estate as security, which creates significant impediments for new businesses.

The procedure of registering a corporation and filing taxes is so intricate and time-consuming that it may be quite demotivating for a newcomer to the country. It would have been more logical if the legislation had been more encouraging and focused on the success of businesses rather than just on how to extract tax from them or how they might be punished. The roots of corruption in public institutions are so deeply ingrained that individuals have lost trust in their ability to achieve larger objectives that are in any way related to the public sector. In Nepal, there is insufficient legislation to safeguard intellectual property rights. Consequently, entrepreneurs and new firms are hesitant to commercialize their ideas and developments because of a lack of solid regulations governing copyright, trademarks, and patents, among other things. Today's youth are drawn to entrepreneurship because of the glitz and glitter that come with it.

The comprehensive approach to entrepreneurship, its lifetime, and its contribution to society and the economy as a whole are all too often disregarded or undervalued. Youths have a strong desire to get wealthy overnight rather than contribute to the industrial sector's general growth. The success of an enterprise is determined not only by its financial success but also by the positive influence it has on people's lives and the progress of a country. This is something that growing adolescents must comprehend. People today seem to be deficient in patience. The desire for short-term success may lead to a concentration on quantitative production, but it may not result in qualitative and long-term success in entrepreneurship. People are more drawn to speculative financial pursuits than they are to taking risks in their daily lives. Incentives are more strongly pushed towards land acquisition, gold and silver savings, building construction, and consumption of luxury goods than they are towards venture capital and new business ventures. As a result, entrepreneurs have difficulty communicating their ideas to others, even their parents. Apart from these, there are other persistent issues, such as political instability, a lack of education and training, an education system that is not based on individual skill development but rather on textbook learning, and so on.,

3.3 Opportunities for Entrepreneurship in Nepal

According to the most recent World Bank annual ranking, Nepal ranks 94th out of 190 nations in the world regarding the ease of doing business in the country[76]. Legal assistance, a suitable atmosphere, a large young population, and an abundance of resources are just a few of Nepal's benefits for boosting entrepreneurship. In terms of commercializing the agriculture sector, Nepal offers tremendous potential. Agriculture is a priority for the Nepali government, which concentrates on modernization, diversification, commercialization, and marketing of the country's agricultural industry Because of increased government assistance for the agricultural industry, businesses will reap more benefits from it. In recent years, there has been a significant increase in tourism. According to the Nepal Tourism Board, the average duration of stay for tourists in Nepal is approximately 13 days.

The majority of Nepal's geographical conditions are conducive to the development of the tourist industry. In Nepal, the information technology industry is seeing significant growth. Information technology offers a strong potential for generating growth, investment, and considerable profits in the entrepreneurship industry. Nepal is a newcomer to information technology entrepreneurship, but it is becoming more significant in contemporary culture[77]. Nepal's IT industry has a more promising future in terms of employment opportunities. It has lower running costs,

---

76 https://data.worldbank.org/indicator/IC.BUS.EASE.XQ
77 https://thehimalayantimes.com/opinion/boosting-entrepreneurshiptarget-the-youth

is more accessible, and has a limited influence on occurrences like the COVID-19 pandemic. There are several issues facing society that need the development of fresh and inventive solutions. Because most young people are focused on studying or working overseas, individuals who opt to remain in the country and develop their entrepreneurial skills have fewer competitors. Beyond these business prospects in Nepal, we still have many challenges to solve, which opens up even more doors for entrepreneurs to pursue their dreams. Finally, we can offer our talents, abilities, and knowledge in Nepal rather than other nations. Even though Nepal faces several obstacles, I believe that this should not serve to discourage the spirit of entrepreneurship in any manner. We do this because embracing challenges and taking risks is fundamental to the very essence of the entrepreneurial spirit itself. Entrepreneurs must have a vision that others do not currently recognize.

People may feel that their ideas are hypothetical and that they impose a high level of uncertainty, but that is what entrepreneurship is all about: putting everything on the line for a hypothesis you believe in. As a result, if we look about, we will see several prospects for entrepreneurial growth in Nepal. There is a catastrophe wherever you look (electricity, water, fuel, communication, inflation). Keep in mind that a crisis may be a window of opportunity for an entrepreneur. Many company concepts may be established here with first-mover advantages since we are still a developing nation and technology is still in its infancy. Because of the high unemployment rate, you may put together a group of determined adolescents anxious to keep their jobs. Even though the world has progressed, there are still many challenges that need fresh and imaginative answers.

The majority of young people are interested in traveling overseas. As a result, people who choose to remain in the area and experiment with entrepreneurial skills have fewer challenges and competition. Because there are fewer development activities in the nation, people with money have fewer sectors in which to invest. Consequently, several investors are eager to invest if an entrepreneur can provide a compelling concept and a viable business plan.

3.4 The Role of Entrepreneurship in making Nepal Successful

There are various reasons why entrepreneurship is vital, ranging from advocating social change to pushing innovation. Most people consider entrepreneurs to be national assets who should be developed, driven, and rewarded to the maximum degree feasible. However, this is not always true. It is indeed true that some of the most industrialized countries, such as the United States, are global leaders thanks to their citizens' innovative and entrepreneurial spirit. Exceptional entrepreneurs can transform the way we live and work on a local and national scale. If they are successful, their ideas may raise living standards. In addition to generating income via entrepreneurial endeavors, they may also provide employment and contribute to the economy's growth as a result of their efforts. Entrepreneurship is very important and should not be underestimated. It is vital because it can raise living standards, generate money for the entrepreneurs themselves, and link firms with the community.

Entrepreneurs also contribute to the advancement of change via innovation, in which new and better goods allow the development of new markets. An excessive amount of entrepreneurship (i.e., a high level of self-employment) may harm economic growth. Entrepreneurial endeavors contribute to the creation of new wealth. Existing enterprises may find themselves restricted to their current markets and at a point of diminishing returns. Entrepreneurs' introduction of new and better goods, services, or technology allows for the development of new markets and new riches.

Increasing employment and higher incomes lead to higher national income via increased tax revenues and government expenditure. The government may use this cash to invest in other suffering industries and human capital if it so chooses. If it results in the layoff of a few current players, the government may mitigate the impact by allocating excess resources to retrain employees.

Chapter 4: What Types of Business Have Scope in Nepal?

Nepal is experiencing widespread problems with power, water, gasoline, communication, and inflation. However, a crisis is an opportunity for an entrepreneur. A crisis can present a chance to become a multi-millionaire while aiding our fellow Nepalis and others in need throughout the world. Startup businesses in Nepal are not for those who lack confidence and assertiveness in their endeavors. Along with the expected uncertainties regarding the demand for your goods and competitors, you'll be entering what may be an entirely new universe, replete with its own business and consumer culture, as well as a distinct language, culture, and way of life.

There are numerous reasons you should consider establishing a business in Nepal. The number of people who have completed formal education is increasing daily, resulting in a higher number of job seekers, people with new and innovative ideas, many of whom are hardworking and enthusiastic people. Working as an entrepreneur in Nepal could potentially enable you to make billions of dollars in several different fields; For example, power, tourism, and agro-based business. Located between two of the world's fastest-growing economies, India and China, Nepal is landlocked. Nepal has the right to special treatment in some lucrative markets since it is a least developed nation. According to investors who have already established themselves in Nepal, two other benefits are the low-cost and non-hostile labor, and a small and easily accessible bureaucracy.

Nepal's natural and cultural resources and its human capital provide investors with very lucrative options. The nation features a diverse spectrum of weather conditions – from tropical to sub-arctic – and a topography that is mountainous in the north, hilly in the center, and close to sea level in the southern regions. As a result, Nepal can produce a wide range of specialist agricultural goods, with medicinal plants and high-quality tea being just two examples. Hydroelectricity has enormous promise in this region. It is estimated that around 44,000 MW is economically possible, contrasting with the approximately 800 MW presently being produced. Despite its enormous potential, Nepal has been unable to realize it fully, and the people of Nepal continue to suffer from acute electricity shortages.

The government is promoting private foreign investment into the hydropower industry to capture and develop energy resources. In recent years, the government has awarded licenses to private sector developers with more than 5000MW of hydropower projects under construction or in different phases of development. These developers include well-known foreign and local companies. Contractors, equipment suppliers, and consultants alike will find tremendous possibilities in this high-priority area. There is potential for foreign investment in a variety of other industries as well. Similarly, the tourism industry has incredible potential. Nepal is blessed with amazing natural resources, including Mount Everest — the highest mountain on the planet – and seven more peaks rising to 8,000 meters or higher[78]. It also boasts a thriving cultural legacy and a diverse range of ethnic communities, each with its customs. Buddha's birthplace is at Lumbini, western Nepal, and Bhaktapur, in Kathmandu valley, is a superbly preserved medieval town rich in Hindu temples. Lumbini is a

---

78 8 Greatest Books on Mount Everest | Nezobooks. https://www.nezobooks.com/best-books-on- mount-everest/

popular tourist destination in Nepal. In Nepal, there are therefore several chances to develop tourism-related ventures, such as hotels and resorts. Other trade potentials also exist, such as telecommunications equipment, information and communications technology equipment, water resources equipment, and airplane components.

The main telecommunications companies are on an expansion spree. Other prospects include civil aviation infrastructure, toll fast track highways, and railroads, to name a few examples. Other industries, such as software development, leather and textiles, pharmaceuticals, electronics, and the service industries, also provide excellent opportunities for foreign investment in the long run.

In addition to medicinal and aromatic herbs, flower and vegetable seeds, floriculture and sericulture, processing of spices, coffee, fruits, and dairy products; vegetable and mushroom farming; and tea, several other sectors offer excellent opportunities for foreign investment. Stone and limestone, talc, silica, dolomite, iron ore, petroleum, and natural gas, are examples of minerals that need additional exploration. Several business options exist in Nepal that have the potential to be profitable, do not be concerned about the shifting political environment. There are always challenges in any given country or region. However, there are a large number of international enterprises operating in the country and producing employment. You may simply develop a business relationship with a Nepalese entrepreneur who will guide you through establishing a new enterprise or collaborating with current firms to grow your future commercial operations in the country.

4.1 Tips for Starting a Business in Nepal

There is a catastrophe wherever you look (electricity, water, fuel, communication, inflation). Remember that a crisis presents an opportunity for an entrepreneur and that you have the potential to become a multi-millionaire while benefiting your fellow Nepalis and others in need throughout the world. Because of the high unemployment rate, you may put together a group of determined adolescents anxious to keep their jobs. Additionally, you get their goodwill and perhaps their loyalty, which will help you develop a viable long-term organization. Corruption may be used by many of your rivals as a means of gaining an advantage in the marketplace. Seize the opportunity presented by this exceptional circumstance and reap the rewards of working in an ethically sound manner.

Understand that those corrupt rivals will never compete with you in terms of openness and honesty (and probably quality also). If your corrupt competitors attempt to outmaneuver you, challenge them to open their accounts and bring the attention of the sensation-hungry media to them, as well as the attention of government watchdogs to their attention.

Nepal is rapidly evolving into a consumer-driven society. We purchase a great deal and discard a great deal. There are opportunities everywhere, from clothing to recycling. Why do you believe there are tens of thousands of families who are committed to recycling our garbage? What do you believe is the reason behind the influx of new stores in malls? Serve our consumer-driven country by providing high-quality products at a competitive price with outstanding customer service! Industries established immediately after civil unrest or conflict may persist for a very long period, as seen by the industries that sprung up after World War II in most of Europe and the United States. So, begin now when there is less competition, to maximize your profits.

4.2 Problems with Starting a Startup in Nepal

Startups are businesses that are formed to test business models that have been built in response to fresh ideas. The word "startup" has been more popular in recent years, particularly in the context of technical initiatives. The startup culture in Nepal is rapidly expanding, with young and dynamic individuals coming up with ground-breaking ideas in the domains of technology and other sectors. Nepal is the finest location in the world to do nearly anything, but there are several difficulties for prospective entrepreneurs when starting their businesses, which has eventually resulted in disheartened and undone entrepreneurs in Nepal today. Many firms attempted to copy Amazon, PayPal, Paytm, Alipay, and Flipkart but failed miserably. The majority of startups do not have a long-term business strategy. Some companies lack a strong sense of direction, and their Profits end up being postponed until the following year.

Such a company model is not sustainable over the long term. Some industries are congested, while others are undercrowded, such as startups in the online retail and food delivery industries. It is possible that using western patterns in the Nepali market may not be successful all of the time. The Nepalese market is distinct. Some firms have been forced to shut due to a misinterpretation of market demands. It has become much too simple to form your own business and appoint oneself as the company's CEO. However, there is a lot more to becoming a great firm than just beginning one. Many firms offer unreasonably low prices to entice users to their products. This results in increased investment in low-profit businesses. Such firms are more prone to experience financial losses, which ultimately lead to their closure, and most startups do not have worthwhile initiatives. Those who are just getting started have been up against players in the market for a long time.

4.3 The Importance of Business Growth in the Progress of Nepal

Nepal is a country that has seen rapid progress in recent years, both domestically and internationally. As a result of the long-awaited political reform, the nation is presently riding high on growth ambitions, fueled by the recent accomplishments it has made in various disciplines. Throughout the process, the government places a high value on development at the local level. It welcomes stakeholders from all over the globe to help it realize its latent economic potential. Nepal is a country that has seen rapid progress in recent years, both domestically and internationally. As a result of the long-awaited political reform, the nation is presently riding high on growth ambitions, fueled by the recent accomplishments it has made in various disciplines. Throughout the process, the government places a high value on development at the local level. It welcomes stakeholders from all over the globe to help it realize its latent economic potential. Some of the most promising investment possibilities and concepts in Nepal include energy from hydropower, renewable energy, and other sources. Due to Nepal's abundance of natural resources, the nation is attractive for possible investment prospects in the global market. Its extensive hydropower resources, including lakes and rivers that run year- round and a large forest cover that provides a good environment, attest to the nation's energy potential. The country is particularly proud of its enormous hydropower resources. Did you know that Nepal's hydropower industry generates about 3% of the world's total electricity generation? These figures demonstrate how much investment potential the nation has in the hydropower industry. The government has been encouraging both national and international partners to participate in its hydroelectric projects to take things a step further.

Among the various initiatives taken by the Nepali government in this regard are the Himalayan Hydropower Expo 2018, which welcomed Bangladeshi investment, the welcoming of foreign investment in mega hydropower projects, the development of national pride projects, and the encouragement of power trading with friendly nations, to name a few. In addition, the nation has been supporting sustainable energy solutions as part of its transition to green cars powered by biofuels, electric vehicles, a drive to eliminate the use of LPG, and a variety of other efforts. Apart from this, the country has been a strong advocate for environmental protection measures through its eco-friendly policies and waste management techniques and through the development of model villages such as Danuta, which have served as classic examples of how to implement such measures successfully. As a result, there is undoubtedly a great deal more that the country's energy industry has to offer prospective investors. Because Nepal is an agriculturally based country, it has tremendous potential in the agricultural sector. All year round, the nation produces a wide variety of crops and is well-known for its traditional types of farming, which are carried out using organic methods.

Most analysts think that agriculture would be one of the most important Nepali industries with significant investment potential over the next twenty to thirty years, given the country's abundant natural resources and expanding middle-class population. The tourism industry is the backbone of the Nepalese economy. Nepal's tourism potential is reflected in the country's traditions, legacy, and world-renowned tourism destinations (some of which are UNESCO World Heritage Sites). Over the years, Nepal has made significant gains in its tourism development, and its *Visit Nepal 2020* campaign currently has a goal of 2 million visitor arrivals by 2020. Under its tourist development objectives, the nation is also interested in creating new areas as tourism centers, which presents an opportunity for prospective investors to capitalize on. Medical tourism is another important sub-area that connects the tourist and healthcare sectors, and it has tremendous potential for growth.

Chapter 5: What is The Role of Businessmen in The Economic Development of Nepal?

Nepali entrepreneurs may be found all over the globe, and the number of them is increasing. Notwithstanding its small size, Nepal is one of the world's least developed nations. However, some wealthy individuals have built their fortunes via commercial ventures in Nepal. Let's look at some of the millionaire and billionaire businesspeople in Nepal, as well as their overall wealth. Having a strong sense of purpose, dedication, and hard effort is essential for achieving success. Money is often seen as a measure of success since it allows people to retain their high social and economic position in every culture across the globe. The best entrepreneurs are held up as identical examples and are compared in terms of their core characteristics. Some Nepalese have altered their fortunes through time due to their hard work, tenacity, and perseverance. These individuals are sometimes referred to as the wealthiest people in the country. There are many successful businesses in Nepal and others who are striving to reach the pinnacle of their respective fields. Several top entrepreneurs in Nepal are achieving great success in their businesses.

5.1 Binod Chaudhary

When you think of a Nepalese entrepreneur, the first name that springs to mind is Binod Chaudhary. But he isn't the only one. He is the first Nepalese to be designated Nepal's first billionaire by Forbes magazine. He serves as the chair of the Chaudhary Group, which consists of around eighty companies and was established on April 14, 1955. Wai Wai Noodles, a product of the Chaudhary Group, are the most successful, with over a billion packages of noodles made yearly and distributed in thirty-five countries worldwide. The banking, cement, real estate, hotels, electronics, home appliances sectors, education, energy, and retail, are some of the other areas in which he has made substantial investments. He founded the Chaudhary Foundation, which is dedicated to the advancement of education, health, and sports. He has also provided scholarships to the less fortunate as well as undertaking projects aimed at improving the educational system and socio-economic conditions in Nepal.

Having grown up at his father's small department store, Binod Chaudhary has contributed to the company's growth into one of Nepal's major firms. Because of his grandfather's assistance, he and his family has grown into one of Nepal's most successful entrepreneurs and he's the 1415th wealthiest person alive, with a net worth of $1.6 billion[79]. The Chaudhary Group owns and operates over eighty businesses spread over five continents, owns, and operates over sixty manufacturing plants in thirty countries, and employs more than six thousand people worldwide. Binod Chaudhary is the most well-known entrepreneur in Nepal, and his name is at the top of the list.

5.2 Min Bahadur Gurung

Have you ever visited the Bhat-Bhateni supermarket in Kathmandu? Do you know who the company's founder is? So, if you've never heard of him before, make a mental note of his surname. Min Bahadur Gurung is his given name. He is the proprietor of the Bhat Bhateni grocery chain,

---

79 https://www.forbes.com/profile/binod-chaudhary/?sh=65b2753a7873

which he founded. Beginning with a single grocery shop with only $1,135, he has grown to have a big number of Bhat-Bhateni franchises that are now spreading across the country and even internationally as well. He serves as an inspiration to future Nepalese entrepreneurs by sharing his remarkable narrative from behind the scenes.

5.3 Ambika Shrestha

Ambika Shrestha is the woman responsible for the success of Dwarika's Hotel. This hotel is one of the most known in the world, and it was built to preserve unique architecture and art in its surroundings. Following her marriage to Dwarika Prasad Shrestha, she relocated to Nepal from her birthplace of Darjeeling, India. Following her husband's death, she assumed entire control of the hotel and helped it reach new heights in the international market. She also serves as the honorary consul general of Spain in Nepal, where she lives. She is one of the most successful female entrepreneurs in Nepal, and she has the potential to encourage more women to become business owners.

5.4 Upendra Mahato

Mr. Upendra Mahato is one of Nepal's most successful businesspeople, and he now resides in Russia. He was born in Siraha, Nepal, in 1960. He has a Ph.D. from the Russian Academy of Sciences. Currently, he serves as president of the Russia-Nepal Chamber of Commerce and Industry[80]. After obtaining his Ph.D., he began working in the business world as an electronic trader. He has since extended his operations to include oil, real estate, banking, and heavy equipment. He is projected to have a fortune in real estate, estimated to be worth a billion dollars. In addition to his commercial endeavors, he has been active in social welfare efforts. In the aftermath of this, he began to broaden the scope of his firm, branching out into industries as varied as electronics and oil. His company employs

80 Top 10 Entrepreneurs of Nepal - Wap Nepal. https://wapnepal.com.np/top-10-entrepre- neurs-nepal/

twelve thousand people and operates in industries like banking, heavy equipment, and real estate, among others. He started as an electronic merchant in Voronezh, where he spent the first several years of his career. He invested in a television plant, which expanded to produce a million TVs each year. In addition to this, he has a television components business that serves eighty thousand customers every day.

Later, Mahato began construction on a high-rise upward-pushing structure suitable for use as a luxury rental block in Moscow. Even though he amassed considerable riches via his commercial endeavors, Mahato's renown is mostly due to his social paintings. Through his many lives, he has developed many health centers in the villages.

5.5 Shesh Ghale

Dr. Shesh Ghale is a successful entrepreneur born and raised in Lamjung, Nepal, based in Melbourne, Australia. He was the 99th wealthiest person in Australia, according to Forbes magazine, and he's the third wealthiest person in Nepal in his current position, he serves as the CEO and founder of the Melbourne Institute of Technology (MIT), which is one of Australia's top private education institutions. He also serves as the president of the National Rifle Association. He received his Master of Civil Engineering degree from the Soviet Union between 1979 and 1986, and he went on to get his MBA from Victoria University in Australia. It was in 1996 that he and his wife co-founded the Melbourne Institute of Technology. Aside from his present involvement in business, he is also interested in the commercial and educational sectors and is the president of the National Rifle Association (Non-Resident Nepali Association).

5.6 Anil Shah

Entrepreneur Anil Shah is widely regarded as one of Nepal's most notable and successful businesspeople. In Nepal, he was the CEO of Mega Bank, which he also founded. His early years saw him rise to the post of chief operations officer in a standard chartered bank, then as CEO of Nabil bank for five years. He established himself as one of the most successful banking figures in a very short time. Within a short period, he is likely to be included among Nepal's most successful businesspeople. He could be one of the most successful instances of new entrepreneurs in the banking industry, if not the most successful. As the CEO of Mega Bank, which is based in Nepal, Anil Shah is a well-known and famous Nepalese entrepreneur who hails from a family of entrepreneurs.

5.7 Birendra Basnet

Birendra Basnet is a name that only a few people are familiar with, but once you get to know him, you will understand who he is. He manages Buddha Air, and he is the managing director. His family came from an agricultural background, and he was the first member of his family to break away from that heritage. The founder of Buddha Air began his firm with a loan fourteen years ago, and now, the company is one of Nepal's most popular and dependable modes of air transportation. He feels that his success has been mostly attributed to his dedication, integrity, and honest conduct. In his family, farming was the way of life, and he was the first member of the family to defy the established order.

5.8 Ajeya Raj Sumargi

Ajeya Raj Sumargi is a well-known figure in Nepali society. He is the founder and chair of the Muktishree group of corporations. He was a founder member of Mero mobile, which is now branded as Ncell, and he served on its board of directors. In his current position, he serves as the executive director of Hello Nepal, which began operations in the Midwestern area and has now extended to include the Far-Western region. He is a pioneering businessperson, manufacturer, and Belarusian ambassador to Nepal, among other things. Ajeya Raj Sumargi net worth is expected to be about 350 million USD[81]. Ajeya Raj Sumargi, his book in which he describes his struggles and experiences, was even released by

---

81 https://www.merokalam.com/top-richest-nepalese/

him in the past year. Ajeya Raj Sumargi is a well-known figure in Nepali society. Arun Raj Sumargi is Ajeya Raj Sumargi's brother, and he writes the foreword of this book. He is one of the most successful industrialists in Nepal, with over thirty-five years of experience in the manufacturing, economics, and agriculture sectors. He is an executive member of Muktishree Group and FNCCI.

5.9 Karna Shakya

Karna Shakya is one of Nepal's most exciting and motivating entrepreneurs, and he has a lot to say about it. A former environmentalist and conservationist who went on to establish his own hotel business and write and give back to the community are among his accomplishments. He has a forestry academic background that he is proud of. Thus, he worked as a wildlife officer and was instrumental in establishing Nepal's first national park, which was established in 1931. His career progressed to include work in the tourist business. He now owns eco-friendly hotels in Kathmandu, Pokhara, Chitwan, and Lumbini, among other locations. He is also a published author of works such as Soch, Khoj, Ma Saxchhu, and Moj. He serves as an inspiration to aspiring entrepreneurs. His novels have served as an inspiration to a large number of Nepalese adolescents. Karna Shakya is one of Nepal's most inspirational and encouraging entrepreneurs. He is also a motivational speaker. In addition to his work as an environmentalist, he has experience as a hotelier, novelist, and philanthropist. He comes from a forestry-related academic background. As a consequence, he became a wildlife officer and played a key role in the establishment of Nepal's first national park in 2017. Later in life, he found employment in the tourist business. He has influenced a large number of Nepalese young entrepreneurs via his novels.

5.10 Balram Chainrai

Mr. Balram Chainrai is the son of Mr. P. G. Chainrai. He was one of the pioneering businesspeople in Hong Kong, along with other national businesses, and was the founding father of the Chainrai institution of companies, which was established in 1949. Mr. Balram received his education in Hong Kong and is conversant in various languages, including Cantonese, English, and Sindhi. Mr. Balram established himself as a significant commercial enterprise figure in Hong Kong quite early in his career. He began his commercial enterprise profession at a young age. In Hong Kong, he established his central enterprise, horning tone enterprises limited, which the establishment of numerous associate organizations quickly followed. The agency is involved in the manufacturing and the purchasing and selling electronic, domestic home equipment and toys; the distribution of computer systems and related add-ons; and the financing of trade transactions. With his active leadership, the commercial company quickly expanded both in terms of enterprise volume and in terms of enterprise variety.

5.11 Savitri Devi Chaudhary

Savitri Devi Chaudhary has risen to important positions in the small business sector in a short period of three years. She is an active member of various organizations and social networks, and she serves as a role model for her town. She is the government member of the District Microentrepreneurs Groups Association (DMEGA), the vice president of the Eastern Regional Micro-Entrepreneurs Federation (ERMEFN), and the executive member of the National Microentrepreneurs Federation Nepal. The proud Savitri adds, "*I had the opportunity to represent my nation as a successful Nepali woman entrepreneur in a fair held in Dhaka, Bangladesh.*"

5.12 Pashupati Shamsher Rana

Pashupati Shamsher Rana was previously referred to as the "King of Entrepreneurs" in Nepal and the "Richest Person in Nepal." He was even regarded to be wealthier than the King. In an interview, he said that his bride, a princess from another country's kingdom at the time, had brought a dowry of 25000 million rupees, which is equivalent to almost $1 billion today.

5.13 Aditya Jha

The entrepreneur, philanthropist, and social crusader Aditya Jha is a Nepalese Canadian who grew up in Canada. In addition to having a $100 million net worth and being a globetrotter, he has an extensive commercial enterprise portfolio that includes multiple startup companies and business turnarounds with activities in Canada, India, Thailand, and Nepal. He also operates various charitable projects via his Charitable Foundation (the POA academic foundation) to boost education and encourage businesses to provide more chances for those who are less fortunate than themself. Through schooling scholarships at top Canadian institutions and a mission that fosters entrepreneurship, Jha is interested in fostering wealth and monetary independence among First Nations communities and individuals in Canada.

Chapter 6: The Economic Environment of Nepal

A tremendous amount of public investment in infrastructure, agriculture, health, and education continues to be required, even in the face of increased access to private capital and pay rises for the poor. Following a twenty-year hiatus, local democracy will be reinstated in the political sphere following the recent municipal elections. Local politicians who have been elected are expected to contribute to the expansion of local development activities. The political parties in Nepal are the most powerful political forces in the country.

It is common for politicians and business executives to have tight working relationships, and political parties have power over trade unions and linkages to civil society groups. Political parties also pick high-level government officials. The civil war and the ethnic uprisings that followed the conflict prompted an ethnically based federal republic. On recent years, a federal compromise map was agreed upon, with provincial elections set to take place in the autumn of that year. There are fears that the ethnic agenda may exacerbate ethnic tensions. It will be vital for all parties to work together to ensure that all social groups are represented inside the newly constituted local units and the economy as whole coming years.

6.1 A Brief Political History of Nepal

The Kingdom of Nepal was established in the eighteenth century when King Prithvi Narayan Shah unified several fiefdoms and tiny kingdoms at the foot of the Himalayas under his reign[82]. A lengthy power battle ensued between the Shah dynasty and the Rana family, culminating in Jung Bahadur Rana's ascent in 1846, who instituted the system of hereditary prime ministers, giving birth to the strong Rana oligarchy. Progressive political and social improvements were attempted occasionally under the Rana dictatorship. Still, conservative forces stopped these attempts within the ruling oligarchy who saw such changes as a danger to their position of power. However, the Rana dynasty finally collapsed under its unpopularity. It was ousted by a coalition of Shah rulers and the Nepalese people in 1951, ushering at the beginning of the modern period in the country.

During the period after the return of the Shah rulers to power, Nepal's politics and economy underwent a significant transformation. People in Nepal saw multi-party democracy for the first time in their history. They watched the first efforts at planned socio-economic growth in the economic realm as well. In 1953, the country's first annual budget was presented, and the country's first development plan was issued the following year, in 1957. Unfortunately, the experiment in multi-party democracy quickly devolved into a power struggle between and within parties, resulting in political instability and the impossibility of implementing long-term economic changes.

Because of increasing political instability, King Mahendra dissolved the democratically elected government of the Nepali Congress Party in 1960 and suspended the parliament, which he condemned. In 1960, he took complete administrative authority and created the Panchayat system, which would become the dominant form of political administration in Nepal for the next three decades. This pseudo-democracy was

---

82 https://www.travelhimalayan.com/nepal-information.php

characterized by the absence of any political parties or ideologies, with people electing their representatives from separate districts individually rather than based on any political theory or party.

Under the leadership of the monarch, the administration implemented a series of social changes, including the updating of the legal code in 1962 and the introduction of land reforms the following year. Pursuing socio-economic growth via five-year development plans, with a particular focus on physical and social infrastructure, was institutionalized and strengthened. Economic policy became more interventionist as the government began to control many critical prices. The monopoly of manufacturing activities was placed in public enterprises, thus prohibiting the development of an independent private sector.

Following the death of King Mahendra, his son, King Birendra, maintained the political-economic system created by his father until the anti-monarchist movement posed a severe threat to his control. Riots erupted, and in a referendum, the people voted to keep the non- party Panchayat system in place, with certain changes. During the next few years, the monarch slowly but steadily loosened his grip on the country's politics and planted the seeds of economic liberalization in Nepal, beginning with the liberalization of the banking and social sectors (especially education). This marked the beginning of a steady reduction in the amount of government interference in the economy.

As far as the political arena was concerned, the authoritarian Panchayat system resulted in the concentration of power on the outskirts of the royal palace. Anger over the abuse of power and alienation felt by ordinary people sparked a new political movement, which saw the Shah family once more unite with the people and successfully establish a constitutional monarchy with a multi-party governmental structure in 1991. Nepal is now a constitutional monarchy with a multi-party government. This shift in the political environment was made possible in part by India, which had placed an economic embargo on Nepal to weaken the dictatorial rule in the country.

The restoration of democracy in 1991 coincided with a sea change in economic policy, with the country moving decisively toward a more liberal economic system and a stronger economic tie with India. However, the re-emergence of inter-party and intra-party feuds, reminiscent of the 1950s, quickly slowed the progress of economic reforms in the country. The inability of major political parties to accommodate the goals of minor political parties has also called into question the very viability of democratic politics in several cases. Political alienation reached its apex in the instance of the Communist Party of Nepal (Maoists), who resorted to military warfare in 1996, which continued to inflict grave wounds on the social fabric for almost a decade after it began.

The Maoist activity started modestly in six districts of the Mid- Western Development Region but gradually extended to almost every section of the nation. Most of the country's most economically backward regions may be found in the Mid-Western Development Region and the Far Western Development Region. They have inherited the worst legacies of the caste system and have been neglected for a long period by administrations of all political colors and political parties. The prevalent poverty in these areas has served as good breeding grounds for the Maoist movement, which thrived for decades. In the year 2020, the number of Maoist assaults on government facilities and persons increased. As a result, the government has resorted to severe measures to quell the rebellion in retaliation. It is estimated that more than seventeen thousand individuals have died due to this war.

In 2002, against a background of rising Maoist insurgency and incessant political wrangling among the major political parties, democracy was struck a fatal blow when the Prime Minister dismissed the parliament and continued to exercise power with the consent of the King of Nepal. An even more devastating blow occurred in February 2002, when King Gyanendra disbanded the coalition government, suspended democracy and civil freedoms, and gained total political authority like that of King Mahendra in 1960, ending the country's democratic tradition. This time, the most significant change was that there were now three political factions, rather than two, vying for dominance and attempting to gain control of the country's governmental institutions. The King, the major political parties, and the Maoists are the three principal players in this conflict. This tri-partite fight for power continued to wreak havoc on Nepalese society until a popular revolt against the King altered the political landscape once again, bringing new hope for political stability to the country for the first time in decades. As a result of the King's powers being severely constrained and the Maoists demonstrating a willingness to integrate into the mainstream political process by avoiding the route of violence, democracy emerged triumphantly.

Considering the political development that has been briefly described above, the history of economic change in contemporary Nepal may be split into four distinct stages. The first phase encompasses the period from the mid-1960s, during which the economy was controlled by the public sector and backed by aggressive development plans. From a political standpoint, the time was marked by an authoritarian Panchayat government coupled with absolute monarchy. From 1981s, the country had a second transitional period marked by the adoption of a liberal Panchayat system, followed by the implementation of outward-oriented economic policies and the steady disintegration of the public sector. During the third phase of the country's history, during 1991, multi-party democracy was reestablished under a constitutional monarchy. A robust program of economic liberalization, privatization, and globalization was implemented, among other things. The fourth and final phase began somewhere around the year 2010. A liberal economic policy was maintained throughout this period. Still, its influence was muted by an all-encompassing political upheaval produced by a protracted tri-partite fight for control.

6.2 Growth and Structure of the Economy

It is estimated that the Nepalese economy increased at an average annual rate of 4 percent throughout the last three decades of the twentieth century. Each capita income climbed at a pace of 1.8 percent per year over the same time, despite the population expanding by 2.2 percent. If this rate of development is averaged across three decades, it equates to a 70 percent improvement in the living standard of the typical Nepali within a generation. Even though this is not a negligible improvement, it represents the slowest rise in per capita income in the whole region of South Asia. The disparity is even starker when comparing Nepal to East and South-East Asia nations, where most countries required just ten to fifteen years to double their per capita GDP. At the same time, Nepal was unable to accomplish this, even after 30 years. When GDP and population both rose at roughly 2.1 percent per year in 2018, the situation was particularly dire, resulting in a standstill in per capita income. There was, however, some progress in the next two decades, during which the economy expanded at a quicker pace of around 5 percent, and per capita income rose at a faster rate of 2.3 percent.

The impetus of this acceleration was continued with the entrance of the twenty-first century, with GDP growth increasing even further to 5.5 percent in 2018 and per capita income growth increasing even further to 3.1 percent. Following that, however, the increase of internal strife and a downturn in the external economic environment caused the economy to suffer a severe blow, from which the nation has not yet recovered. Nepal's economy increased at around the same pace throughout both 2017 and 2020 (approximately 5 percent) when it comes to growth rates. Still, the proximate sources of development were different between the two decades. The agricultural sector was primarily responsible for the improvement in growth that happened in 2017 compared to 2018. Agriculture had experienced a dreadful decade in 2018, with a growth of less than 2 percent in the first half of the decade and negative growth in the second half of the decade. However, there was a big reversal in 2017, when agricultural growth increased to around 4.5 percent, far outpacing the pace of population growth, which was 2.3 percent. A decline in the state of agriculture began again. While the situation improved significantly in the second half of the decade, the average growth rate for the decade dropped to about half of the pace obtained in 2017 throughout the decade. However, total GDP growth was sustained during 2020 due to increased performance in non-agricultural sectors, particularly manufacturing. This has resulted in huge structural changes in the Nepalese economy, which are still being felt today. Agriculture used to account for more than 70 percent of the country's gross domestic product (GDP) about 2015. By 2020, it had reduced its market share to slightly about 40 percent of the total.

On the other hand, the manufacturing sector rose from a meager 4 percent of the economy in 2015 to more than 9 percent in 2020, a significant gain. Other non-agricultural businesses, such as construction, commerce, transportation, finance, and real estate, have also seen significant increases in their percentage of GDP during the previous two and a half decades, as has the share of agriculture. In Nepal, an effort at growth accounting has recently been made, which has cast more light on the proximal drivers of development (Khatiwada and Sharma, 2019). Recent research discovered that the increased production was mostly due to capital accumulation rather than labor accumulation.

On the other hand, total factor productivity did not make a significant contribution to the growth process. As a result, total factor productivity has dropped over the last two decades, reducing rather than increasing the rate of economic development. The drop in total factor productivity, on the other hand, was restricted to 2017. A significant improvement occurred in before COVID, when total factor productivity made a positive, if the small, contribution to the rise of production, accounting for 10 percent of the increase in output. Indeed, the increase in remittances has been one of the most important developments in the Nepalese economy in recent years, and it is expected to continue. Since early years, the magnitude of remittances has increased at an astonishingly fast pace of 30 percent per year, with significant implications for economic development, poverty alleviation, and inequality reduction. Around 2020, over 800,000 employees have worked abroad, mostly in India, and their remittances amounted to approximately 12 percent of the country's gross domestic product. It is worth noting that, remittances contributed more to foreign currency profits ($800 million) than both goods exports ($633 million) and tourism ($155 million), providing a comparative perspective on the significance of remittances for the Nepalese economy.

During 2017, public investment accounted for the majority of the rise in investment, supported largely by greater inflows of foreign assistance and augmented by growing reliance on deficit financing. From around 4 percent of GDP in 2018 to more than 7 percent in 2017, public investment grew rapidly. Although private investment grew somewhat throughout this period, it was still just a minor rise. Although state investment stalled, private investment began to gain speed in Nepal throughout recent years. For the first time in its history, there were indications of private investment gaining momentum even as public investment remained stagnant. The percentage of private investment in GDP has increased to 14 percent in the last decade, up from an average of 11 percent during the previous decade. While the rate of governmental investment remained static throughout 2020, only the increase of private investment allowed the total investment rate to continue to rise during that period. However, since the overall investment environment worsened around the turn of the century due to the increase of Maoist insurgency and the global economic slump, private investment fell and has only slowly recovered in recent years.

6.3 Trends of GDP

The failure of the Nepalese government to produce sufficient domestic money has had a significant impact on the country's budgetary operations. In 1998, It was barely 7 percent of GDP that the government collected as taxable income. Approximately two decades later, in 2020, this percentage had gradually increased to 10 percent. Meanwhile, government spending increased at a significantly quicker rate, rising from 11 percent of GDP to 17 percent of GDP. Initial increases in spending were primarily motivated by the need to spend more money on infrastructure for economic and social growth and other things. Development spending as a percentage of GDP climbed from 8.7 percent in the second half of 2017 to 12.6 percent in 2018 due to this transformation. However, the percentage of development spending began to drop after that, partially due to the increasing demands on resources that came about as a result of the necessity to cope with the insurgency crisis. By the turn of the twenty-first century, the percentage of development spending in GDP had decreased even more, to levels comparable to those seen in 2018.

While Nepal received international assistance for the majority of this period, the country's development spending was mostly funded by domestic sources. It was the growing supply of assistance that made it feasible to increase the proportion of domestic money spent on development even when domestic revenue growth remained slow. The amount of foreign assistance climbed from 4.1 percent of GDP in late 2018 to 7.6 percent of GDP in late 2017: a significant rise. On the other hand, when it came to foreign aid, the pattern was the same as development expenditure: it rose in 2017 and fell in 2020. This pattern in foreign aid was fully reflected in the trend in development expenditure, which followed the same time path – rising in 2017 and falling in the following years. Development spending has therefore been squeezed on two fronts in recent years: on the one hand, as a result of the fall in the relative magnitude of foreign assistance, and on the other, as a result of the diversion of resources caused by the rise of the Maoist insurgency. In 2017, the need to increase development investment in the face of weak income growth resulted in fiscal imbalances, which had major ramifications for the country's overall macroeconomic situation. Budget deficits increased, reaching 6.5 percent of GDP: a significant increase from the average deficit of 2.2 percent of GDP that prevailed throughout 2018.

More significantly, the proportion of the deficit funded domestically increased dramatically, rising from 1.1 percent of GDP in 2017 to 2.8 percent of GDP in 2018. Increased deficit financing resulted in inflation and balance of payments challenges, prompting a series of economic reforms aimed at restoring macroeconomic stability while also stimulating economic development to be implemented. In the sense that budget deficits were reduced, as were inflation and the balance of payments deficits, these changes were most effective in eliminating macroeconomic imbalances; nevertheless, their success in stimulating economic development remains a topic of contention. Due to Nepal's dependence on foreign assistance as the principal source of funding for its expanding development spending, its indebtedness has increased on a large scale. In late 2017, the outstanding amount of foreign debt represented just 5 percent of the country's GDP. In late 2018, this ratio had risen to 29 percent, and in late 2020, it had risen even more to 52 percent. Thank goodness for soft loans, since most of this debt has been kept within acceptable boundaries by their low-interest rates and short payback terms. While these improvements have been made, the debt-servicing ratio (loan repayments as a proportion of export profits) has increased dramatically, rising from 3.5 percent in 1984/85 to 9.3 percent in 2020/21. The most alarming part of the debt load, on the other hand, is the strain it puts on the government's budget. When internal and external debt is combined, the repayment burden consumes more than a quarter of overall government income, increasing from less than a fifth in mid-2017 to more than a quarter now. When looking at the debt load, it's also worth noting that the total repayments of internal and external debt account for more than half of overall development spending. In 2020, loan repayments amounted to around 56 percent of total development expenditure when it came to development spending. As a result, Nepal's debt crisis is more of a fiscal problem than a balance of payments concern, but it is still a very significant problem. The failure of Nepal's government to generate sufficient money throughout the years has been the primary cause of the country's massive debt burden to pay its development spending. Following the implementation of a series of fiscal reforms by the government in the first half of 2020, there was an increase in revenue growth.

However, this increase did not continue long, with the growth rate falling by almost half in the second half of the decade. The government collected just 11 percent of GDP in revenue by 2020 while spending 17 percent. Similar to the majority of other developing nations, indirect taxes provide for the vast majority of income. According to the CIA, until the mid-2020, their percentage of overall income stayed relatively stable at approximately 65 percent, after which it decreased to less than 60 percent. In addition, several modifications have occurred in the composition of indirect taxes. Customs duties' percentage of total income decreased significantly from 29 percent to 25 percent during 2020, when tariffs were lowered, and trade liberalization was pushed with considerable vigor. However, the share of sales taxes' part of total revenue climbed from 18 to 24 percent over the same period. Direct taxes presently account for over one-fifth of total revenue, which is a significant amount.

In comparison to the previous two decades, when the percentage of direct taxes remained almost unchanged at roughly 14 percent, this constitutes an improvement. It wasn't until the second half of 2020 that there was a significant increase in the collection of direct taxes in Nepal. In addition, the structure of public spending has changed little throughout the years. The most significant shifts are the growing proportions of social services and debt payment on the one hand and the decreasing percentages of economic services on the other.

The reallocation of public expenditure from the economic to the social sectors is consistent with the stated goal of previous budgetary reforms, which was to direct more resources to the social sectors via increased allocation of resources. Following economic liberalization and privatization, the justification for this plan was that the private sector would take care of the economic sectors, which has been supported by the evidence. Since 2018, when the reform programmers were launched in earnest, the allocation to economic sectors has risen at a rate that is 50 percent faster than the allocation to economic services, according to the International Monetary Fund. Taking a longer-term perspective, the percentage of social services in total public spending has increased from 23 percent to 30 percent in the twenty years since the second half of 2018. During the same period, the proportion of economic services has decreased from 51 percent to 35 percent. Perhaps too extreme has been the fall in the percentage of economic sectors, resulting in a stall in public investment, even before the escalation of the economic and social crises that happened at the turn of the twenty-first century. Stagnant public investment in critical economic infrastructure will hurt Nepal's capacity to create sustainable development in the future.

Only a portion of the drop in the percentage of economic sectors can be ascribed to purposeful choices between social services and other economic sectors — about around half of the fall in the share of economic sectors. The second factor is the increasing strain of repaying previous debts, which is a contributing factor. The proportion of overall public spending devoted to debt payment has climbed dramatically, rising from less than 5 percent in late 2018 to about 15 percent in late 2020. Accordingly, it is possible to argue that Nepal's ability to maintain acceptable levels of expenditure on economic sectors while increasing the share of social sectors is primarily due to the legacy of excessive borrowing in the past, which supports the claim that debt burden has emerged as a serious fiscal concern in the country earlier this year. One good feature of Nepal's financial allocation has been the government's focus on priority sectors in social expenditures, which has been a source of pride for the country. When measured against the benchmark of the "20/20-compact," which envisions 20 percent of government spending being allocated in social priority sectors, with an equivalent proportion of donor money to supplement this allocation, it seems that the trend in budgetary allocation is in the correct direction. The allocation to social priority sectors from the government's resources grew from 8.3 percent of overall budgetary spending in 1976 to 17 percent in 2018, representing 8.3 percent in 1976. In addition, the percentage of contributors' contributions increased from 7.5 percent in 1993 to 15 percent in 2018. Other parts of financial allocation, on the other hand, have fallen well short of the worldwide standards that have been established. Examples include that, in the early years of the present decade, the percentage of total budgetary spending in GNP stayed around 20 percent, when the mandated standard is 25 percent. Additionally, the social sector allocation ratio was 31 percent, compared to the needed ratio of 40 percent for the sector.

Furthermore, the priority sector allocation ratio, which had stayed stable at good levels until late 2020, began to decline in the following years. Accordingly, human development investment has decreased, accounting for just 15 percent of total public expenditure and 3 percent of the gross national product (GNP) in 2020, against the recommended levels of 20 percent and 5 percent, respectively. During the last decade and a half, the government of Nepal has made explicit efforts to influence public spending in a pro-poor direction, with varying degrees of success. It has been estimated that around one-third of overall public expenditure goes toward anti-poverty initiatives. Furthermore, social services account for one-third of total expenditure, with more than half of that amount going to the social priority sectors. At the same time, fiscal decentralization has been explored as a proactive mechanism for boosting pro-poor expenditure and investment in infrastructure.

6.4 Nepal's Economic Crisis

In an article written by Hari Bansh Jha for the Observer research foundation[83], reported that the 29-million-person Himalayan country of Nepal has likely never previously seen an economic crisis this severe, both internally and outside. The country is in a crisis on the international front as a result of diminishing remittances, a growing trade deficit brought on by an extraordinary increase in imports, skyrocketing balance of payments imbalances, and dwindling foreign exchange reserves[84]. On the home front, the cost of necessities has skyrocketed, and banks no longer offer loans for the majority of commercial endeavors. Due to some of these economic problems, many Nepalis are concerned that their country may be headed in the same route as Sri Lanka, where the pre- economic crisis symptoms were just as pronounced as they are now.

However, the Communist Party of Nepal - Maoist Centre (CPN-MC), led by Pushpa Kamal Dahal and simple politician Janardan Sharma, who has any economic expertise, has rejected that Nepal is experiencing a serious economic crisis. Despite these assertions, many have begun pressuring him to step down because of his inability to confront the economic crisis. The conflict between the country's Finance Minister and Central Bank Governor is already evidence of the economic crisis.

The Governor of Nepal Rastra Bank, the nation's central bank, was suspended after Minister Sharma occasionally accused him of "incompetence, leaking secret information, and failing to fulfill his responsibilities" in an effort to draw attention away from himself.

---

83 https://www.orfonline.org/expert-speak/nepals-economic-crisis/
84 Is Nepal the Next Sri Lanka? - intpolicydigest.org. https://intpolicydigest.org/the-platform/is- nepal-the-next-sri-lanka/

This prompted questions about the government's dedication to preserving the independence of the nation's central bank. His suspension by the Finance Minister was only overturned, and he was sent back to work thanks to the Supreme Court of Nepal's intervention.

The fight between the nation's Finance Minister and Central Bank Governor is already evidence of the economy's problems. According to recent data, the country's inflation rate has soared to 7.14 percent, mostly as a result of an increase in transportation and building expenditures. Additionally, investors' faith in the economy has been damaged by the 41.77 points decline in the rate of the Nepal Stock Exchange.

The banks and other financial institutions are finding it more and more difficult to lend money, even to productive industries like manufacturing, agriculture, tourism, and the energy industry. In mid-August/mid-September of 2021, the banks provided INR 187 billion in loans, but by mid-January/mid-February of 2022, that amount had sharply dropped to INR 11 billion. The impact of the conflict in Ukraine, which raised the price of gasoline and various agricultural items, has had a significant influence on the economy's growth rate.

The macroeconomic growth rate, which the World Bank had previously anticipated to reach 7%, has now been reduced to 3.7%. The impact of the conflict in Ukraine, which raised the price of gasoline and various agricultural items, has had a significant influence on the economy's growth rate. In the previous fiscal year, the nation bought oil worth INR 175.53 billion; however, in just eight months this year, the imports of oil increased to INR 184.98 billion.

Despite its reputation as an agricultural nation, Nepal has imported an increasing amount of food grains throughout time. Compared to the prior year, 2019–20, Nepal's imports of food and agricultural goods from India alone increased by 38.9 percent in 2020–21. The nation brought in 1.2 million tons of rice for $402.91 million in 2020– 21.

The trade imbalance increased to a level of US$ 9.5 billion in the first eight months of the current fiscal year as a result of the sharp increase in imports, which is almost the whole amount of the Government of Nepal's budget. In addition, the nation's foreign exchange reserves have decreased noticeably, falling by more than 18% from US$ 12 billion in the first eight months of the previous fiscal year in 2021–22 to US$ 9.6 billion in the same time of the current fiscal year in 2021–22[85]. The current level of foreign exchange reserve, which cannot maintain imports for more than almost six months, is a subject of grave worry at a time when the government is in desperate need of foreign exchange to pay for the debt, given the debt service ratio of US$ 333 million.

In order to combat the economic crisis, the Government of Nepal received a US$ 659 million grant from the US government through USAID for the construction of infrastructures, such as roads and electrical transmission lines, over a five-year period. Also prohibited from opening letters of credit for the importation of luxury items like automobiles and cosmetics are the traders. The government cut its spending on fuel for departments, agencies, and public companies by 20%.

In order to reduce oil demand and consumption, the administration is also thinking of implementing a two-day weekend program. As if this is not enough, the government decreased expenditure on gasoline for government agencies, ministries, and public corporations by 20 percent. In a desperate attempt to raise money, the administration also made a plea to the Nepalese diaspora abroad to open dollar accounts and invest in Nepal.

The effectiveness of the following actions taken by the Government of Nepal to solve the economic crisis, which is escalating day by day, would only become apparent with time. Despite the possibility that some of the government's actions might lower imports and, to some extent, halt the loss of foreign exchange reserves, there is a significant concern that they

---

85 Is Nepal the Next Sri Lanka? - intpolicydigest.org. https://intpolicydigest.org/the-platform/is- nepal-the-next-sri-lanka/

would have an adverse impact on tax collection. Given that the country only has a small number of exportable goods, there are very few odds that exports will increase, at least in the near future.

In order to strengthen its foreign exchange reserves, the government's sole remaining alternative is to draw in foreign direct investment (FDI), resuscitate the tourist sector, and implement the Millennium Challenge Corporation agreement (MCC). The Nepali diaspora should be encouraged to contribute money to Nepal through the financial system and to invest in profitable industries by engaging with diplomatic missions abroad, especially in wealthy nations like the USA, UK, Australia, Japan, South Korea, Canada, Hong Kong, and Europe. If this were to happen, Nepal might prevent itself from going through a serious economic catastrophe like Sri Lanka, which has been plagued by depleted foreign exchange reserves.

Chapter 7: Money, Inflation, and Growth in Nepal

The conduct of monetary policy in Nepal is severely hampered due to the country's fixed exchange rate system. The Nepalese government has maintained a policy of fixed peg and free convertibility between its currency and other countries' currencies to allow free and developing commerce with India. In the process, however, Nepal's monetary sovereignty has been severely restricted. For this reason, Nepal's interest rates must be tightly aligned with Indian rates to prevent any destabilizing capital flight between the two nations, which is now taking place. Historically, Nepal has pursued a strategy of keeping its deposit rates somewhat higher than India's to prevent money from leaving the country. However, as a result of the financial liberalization that has occurred, there has been a mismatch between the interest rate structures of Nepal and India. This has been the case, when interest rates in India have tended to rise, while in Nepal they have tended to fall, primarily as a result of excess liquidity in the banking system, which has been caused primarily by higher volumes of capital inflow. Thus, Nepalese interest rates stayed lower than those in India as a consequence of this. Given that this disparity in interest rates created a danger of capital flight towards India, Nepalese banks have been increasing their deposit rates to bring them into line with those of other countries. As a result of these modifications, the deposit rate structure in Nepal has been brought back into line with that of India on the whole.

While Nepal has seen mild inflation, the country has also experienced periodic volatility, which is comparable to the experience of the rest of South Asia. During the previous three and a half decades, the average annual inflation rate was around 9 percent. As recently as the 1960s, the inflation rate was relatively modest, running about 5 percent on average. After being propelled into double-digit digits for the first time by the oil crisis of early 2008, inflation in Nepal retreated to the 5 percent threshold by the end of that decade. After 2017, Nepal underwent what may be defined as a period of relatively high inflation. During the early part of 2017, the Nepal ran large budget deficits, which ushered in this period of high inflation. Inflation was influenced by both direct and indirect consequences of deficit finance. The direct impact was felt as a result of the rise of surplus demand due to the budget deficits that were incurred. The balance of payments was the conduit via which the indirect impact was felt. Because of the inflationary pressures created by excess demand, the country had a balance of payments deficits in mid- 2017, which required a 15 percent devaluation in late 2017, which fueled increased inflationary pressure in the second half of the decade. Inflation remained high in Nepal throughout the first half of 2020, partly because of a 21 percent devaluation necessitated by a comparable devaluation by India, with whom Nepal has significant economic relations, and in part because of a devaluation by Nepal. It wasn't until that the pace of inflation started to decline significantly. It is particularly noteworthy that the pricing situation has improved significantly in recent years. Inflation has averaged 3.7 percent, compared to an average of 9.3 percent in the second half of 2020 throughout the same period. It is believed that the current fall in inflation is partly due to lower import costs and partly due to the slowdown in the country's economic growth.

Nepal and India have a long and open border, allowing for the free movement of goods and services over the border based on the free convertibility of the two countries' currencies. Cross-border flows of daily-consumption products contribute to the equalization of cross- border pricing differences. Therefore, the low food costs that have lately prevailed in India have resulted in lower food prices being experienced in Nepal as well. Since recent years, low inflation has been a consequence of a combination of factors, including weak domestic demand for non- food commodities due to the economic slump. In 1950, Nepal was just starting on the road of modern economic growth. At the time, India was Nepal's practically exclusive commercial partner, accounting for more than 95 percent of its commerce. Even though India continues to be Nepal's most important trading partner, the country's trade system has undergone significant diversification over time. The fixed exchange rate policy and free convertibility of the rupee with other currencies, together with a vast and porous border between India and Nepal, have contributed to the country's continued dominance in international commerce. However, there was a progressive drop in the significance of India as a trade partner, with India's portion of Nepal's exports and imports falling to barely 15 percent and 33 percent, respectively, of Nepal's total exports and imports. As a result of the new Commerce Treaty negotiated between India and Nepal in 1996, which further liberalized trade, this tendency was reversed after the 1999. The most current Indo-Nepal Treaty, which was extended in 2019, has imposed additional limitations, including stricter rules of origin requirements and paperwork, as well as trade- related limits triggered by the number of goods exported. Nonetheless, India accounts for almost half of Nepal's total exports and imports at the moment. Furthermore, India plays a significant role in Nepal's foreign transactions not only in terms of physical trade but also in terms of financial transactions.

More than one-third of Nepal's foreign direct investment (FDI) is in joint ventures with India, and more than 70 percent of the country's foreign labor force is employed in India. As a result, remittance income, which has come to play such a significant role in the Nepalese economy, is derived primarily from India. Nepal has seen tremendous gains in the volume of its international commerce, which has coincided with the diversity of its trading partners. When expressed as a percentage of GDP, Nepal's trade ratio expanded from 19 percent in the second half of 2018 to about 40 percent, making it one of the most open economies in South Asia. Both exports and imports have seen substantial growth, with the latter growing at a far quicker rate. The ratio of exports to GDP has almost doubled in the last four decades. On the other hand, the trade deficit surged dramatically from 7 percent in the second half of 2018 to 21 percent in the second half of 2020 before declining significantly to 15 percent. Although the trade deficit has grown since 2018, the current account has improved due to increased contributions from service and transfer revenue, particularly from workers' remittances.

Aside from that, the overall balance of payments has stayed in surplus for most of the period, resulting in a substantial cushion of foreign currency reserves. Over many decades, the structure of Nepal's exports has experienced substantial alteration. It is the increasing significance of manufactured exports that stands out as the most striking element. It is worth noting that between 2017 and 2018, the percentage of primary products exports decreased from roughly 70 percent to 17 percent, but the share of manufactured exports climbed from 30 percent to 75 percent over the same time. Despite this, it must be acknowledged that Nepal's export industry is plagued by major structural problems that must be addressed. As previously stated, the primary concern is that the export business is very tightly focused on only three product categories - apparel, carpets, and pashmina wool. These three categories accounted for almost 50 percent of total export revenues in 2018. As a result of the high degree of market concentration that characterizes Nepalese exports, the nation is particularly exposed to external shocks.

7.1 Poverty and Inequality

Nepal is one of the world's poorest nations. However, there is evidence that poverty has been falling in recent years. Nepal is one of the poorest countries in the world[86]. Because of a lack of comparable data, it is impossible to determine the pattern that will persist over a longer period. Data from household income and expenditure surveys conducted in rural regions in 1976/77, 1984/85, 1991, 1995/96, and 2020/21 were used to calculate poverty estimates in the real world. However, since the only comparable figures are those produced from the most recent two polls, it is impossible to determine any long-term trend from these data. Because of the non-comparability of data, it is preferable to investigate the development of poverty in Nepal in two stages: first, for the time before 1995, and then for the period after 1995. World Bank (2020) attempted to obtain comparable estimates of poverty over time for the period before 1995 by using the same definitions of the poverty line, income, and consumption across all of the surveys. Because the definitions used in the Nepal Living Standards Survey of 1995/96 are in many ways superior to those used earlier, it would have been ideal for applying these definitions to the earlier data sets; however, this was not possible due to a lack of raw data from the earlier surveys at the time of the survey.

Consequently, the researchers had to settle for the less desirable strategy of applying the criteria used in prior polls to the data from 1995/96, which were less satisfactory. At the very least, this approach had the advantage of producing estimates at various times that were similar to one another. The first set of poverty estimates is based on existing poverty figures from 1976/77. The second set of poverty estimates is based on the definitions used in the 1976/77 survey to create similar poverty estimates

---

86 Nixon, Cath. "Member Appeals for Nepal Victims." Community Practitioner, vol. 88, no. 6, Redactive Publishing Ltd., June 2015, p. 8.

for 1995/96. It is possible to create similar Poverty Estimates for 1995/96 by using existing Poverty Estimates from 1984/1985 and applying the definitions used in the 1984/1985 survey to get comparable Poverty Estimates from 1995/96. As a result, the first group allows us to compare 1976/77 with 1995/96, while the second set allows us to compare 1984/85 with 1995/96. The most startling finding to emerge from these figures was that the incidence of poverty in Nepal grew significantly between 1976/77 and 1995/96, rising from 33 percent to 42 percent over this period.

However, even though the precise statistics are not credible due to the problematic criteria employed, one may have greater confidence in the direction of change reflected by the data. Also apparent is a significant increase in poverty, much above any reasonable margin of error that might have resulted from sampling and non-sampling causes. In addition, the deepening of poverty was mostly a rural phenomenon, which is worth noting in its own right. Urban poverty seems to have decreased, if only somewhat, in recent years. The third issue worth mentioning is that the worsening of rural poverty seems to have happened mostly in the decade before 1984/85 rather than after. This is shown by the fact that rural poverty increased very little between 1984/85 and 1995/96, indicating that the situation has improved. Furthermore, the marginal improvement in urban poverty that has been recorded since 1977 seems to have happened mostly after 1984/85, rather than before. Overall, the Nepalese economy looks to have done better on the poverty front in the decade after 1984/85 than in the decade before that.

According to the comparison between 1991 and 1995/96, the second half of the period showed improved performance on poverty issues. The World Bank (2020) discovered that rural poverty decreased somewhat and, at worst, did not increase during the first half of 2020 by applying consistent criteria to data from the 1991 Rural Credit Survey and the 1995/96 Living Standard Survey. After further investigation, it was discovered that primarily the rural regions around the Kathmandu valley and the rural Terai (southern plains) region saw improvements in 2020. In contrast, the remainder of rural Nepal had a decline in living standards during this period. It is possible to sum up the general pattern that emerges from the facts provided above: From 2015 forward, the Nepalese economy saw rapid expansion while mostly ignoring its most vulnerable sectors, the rural poor. The urban sector saw some improvement, and the growing urban economy may have had a positive spill-over effect on some neighboring rural areas. Still, the rest of rural Nepal saw poverty increase in 2007 and, at best, remained unchanged in the following decade, according to the World Bank. The pace of agricultural expansion was just more than the rate of population increase, which was 2.6 percent per year.

Consequently, it should come as no surprise that rural poverty increased throughout this time as well. In contrast, the non-agricultural sector in cities increased at a respectable rate, at least after 2017. As a consequence, urban poverty decreased to a certain amount throughout this period. It is conceivable to suggest that urban poverty would have fallen by far greater margin if rural-to-urban migration had not been so prevalent. However, the same migratory phenomena, in conjunction with other trickle-down processes, has also resulted in rural communities in the proximity of rising urban centers (mostly in the Kathmandu valley) being able to benefit from the development process as a result of the process. However, the trickle-down impact of urban-biased development was much too weak to make any significant dent in rural poverty in other parts of the world. The image for the post-1995 era is much more solidly founded since data from the similar Living Standard Surveys of 1995/96 and 2020/04 can be utilized to establish consistent estimates of poverty in the Nepal and other countries. Between 1995/96 and 2020/04, estimates generated by applying the same approach to data from these two polls suggest that poverty has decreased significantly, with the headcount ratio falling from 42 percent to 31 percent between the two surveys. It was particularly noticeable in metropolitan areas, where poverty was more than halved within eight years, with the headcount ratio dropping from 22 percent to 10 percent in only eight years.

Poverty dropped less rapidly in rural regions – from 43 percent to 35 percent – but the magnitude of the reduction was still significant, particularly when compared to the evidence of growing rural poverty over the two decades between the mid-2018 and mid-2020. When compared to the national account's figures, one obvious flaw in these estimates is that the scale of poverty reduction seems to be considered too dramatic compared to the national account's statistics. For the simple reason that household surveys, based on which poverty estimates are developed, suggest that private consumption has improved far more than indicated by national accounts figures, this is the case. The national accounts figures indicate, for example, that real per capita private consumption increased by 12 percent between 1995/96 and 2020/04. Still, household survey data suggest that real per capita private consumption increased 42 percent during the same time.

Consequently, if one were to base one's assessment just on national accounts statistics, the level of poverty reduction would seem to be greatly exaggerated. The real rate of increase in private consumption would be larger than what the national accounts disclose, even if it were not as high as survey-based estimates, which is a moot point, given there are no compelling reasons to think such. First and foremost, the GDP growth rate of Nepal is regarded to be understated, particularly in businesses like commerce, construction, livestock, and dairy products, which are all seeing rapid expansion.

What's more, official national income figures do not fully account for the increase in remittances sent home by Nepalese employees employed overseas. With remittances accounting for as much as 12 percent of Nepal's GDP in 2019/03, they have risen to a significant position in its economy. They have likely played a significant part in the country's poverty reduction efforts. The rise in remittances began to accelerate, and household surveys are likely to capture this development far more accurately than national income statistics. As a result, the velocity with which poverty has fallen is not as unrealistic as it would seem at first glance.

Furthermore, estimates of subjective poverty, which are generated from perception data acquired by the same household surveys, show a nearly equal amount of decrease. Objective estimates of rural earnings also show that the living standards of the poor have improved throughout the country. All things considered, although the accuracy of poverty figures may be called into question, there is no reason to dispute that Nepal has seen a significant reduction in poverty over the previous decade. The fall in poverty has been impressively broad-based, if not uniform, across occupational, geographical, and ethnic boundaries After 1995/96, people in all types of vocations, including the self-employed and wage earners, agriculturists, and those in the industrial and service industries, saw a reduction in poverty levels.

The sole exception was landless agricultural laborers, who accounted for around 10 percent of Nepal's labor force and whose poverty levels stayed constant throughout the decade. Each of the country's five so- called "development areas" have seen a decrease in poverty levels during the last decade. A reduction in poverty has also been observed across regional boundaries, with the fastest reduction in poverty occurring in the region that had the highest incidence of poverty in 1995/96 (the Far- Western region) and the slowest reduction occurring in the region that had the lowest incidence in 1995/96 (the Southern region).

A similar pattern can be seen in the country's three ecological belts: the Terai (southern plains), the Hills, and the Mountains (or the Himalayas). It was formerly believed that regional poverty in Nepal varied directly with altitude, with the lowest levels found on the plains, somewhat higher levels found in the Hills, and the greatest levels found in the Mountains. Although this common knowledge seemed to be genuine until 1995/96, it seems to have been debunked in recent years. In 1995/96, the incidence of poverty in the Mountains was much higher than in the Terai and Hills, with 57 percent compared to slightly over 40 percent in the Terai and Hills. However, it was over the following eight years that poverty in the Mountains was reduced at the greatest rate, to the point, the extent of poverty in this belt (33 percent) was somewhat lower than in the Hills (35 percent) and not much greater than in the Terai (28 percent). But it should be emphasized that a slightly different categorization of areas reveals portions of the nation that did not contribute to the general decrease in poverty. Those living in the Rural Eastern Hills, on the other hand, have had the opposite experience, with poverty increasing in this region from 36 percent in 1995/96 to 43 percent in 2020/04. There is a possibility that this deviation from the usual trend is due at least in part to the geographical distribution of remittances. Notably, this is the only area in Nepal that has decreased the flow of remittances, while all other regions have seen a rise in varying degrees.

7.2 Evolution of Poverty

Reduced poverty between 1995/96 and 2020/04 was rather broad- based, benefitting people from all areas and various occupational and ethnic backgrounds, with the majority of people benefiting from the decrease in poverty. In reality, the most impoverished areas had the fastest reductions in poverty, resulting in a trend of convergence across the regions regarding its prevalence. There were a few things that were a little off-putting, however. Landless agricultural laborers were the only occupational category to benefit little from the process of poverty reduction. Within ethnic groupings, those from the lower castes profited far less than those from the higher castes, in contrast to the overall trend.

When examining the factors that contributed to the fall in poverty in Nepal after 1995, it is useful to focus on rural poverty in particular, since rural Nepal had a spectacular reversal of trend after 1995, as previously stated. Examining the origins of rural income development, particularly the sources of rising income of the rural poor, might provide valuable insights. The most surprising conclusion is that virtually all of the rise in income that the poor rural saw between 1995/96 and 2020 came from two sources, both of which are located outside of agriculture, which is the primary source of subsistence for the vast majority of the rural poor in Nepal. A total of 51 percent of the incremental income of the rural poor came from non-agricultural wage income, with remittances accounting for 49 percent of the total. Agriculture, on the other hand, had a net negative contribution to the economy. The fall in rural poverty after 1995, it would seem, had nothing to do with what was occurring in rural Nepal at the same time.

The spillover impact of the fast expansion of the non-agricultural sector was the most beneficial to the rural poor. A similar spill-over impact occurred, as previously mentioned, although it was restricted mostly to the Kathmandu valley and its environs at that period. With the expansion of non-agricultural enterprises after 1995, rural poor people in most regions of the nation could participate in wage labor outside of agriculture for the first time. The influx of remittances was nearly as significant as the influx of tourists. According to the Living Standard Surveys, the proportion of households receiving remittances increased from 23 percent in 1995/96 to 32 percent in 2020/04, and, more significantly, per capita remittances increased by more than 150 percent in real terms during this period.

Furthermore, semi-urban and rural regions benefited from this windfall just as much as urban areas in Nepal. The direct advantage of remittances for the Kathmandu area was less than the national average — the rest of Nepal benefited more than the Kathmandu region. In this way, the combined impact of remittances and greater job possibilities created by the non-agricultural sector may be attributed to Nepal's achievement in decreasing poverty throughout rural areas after 1995.

While poverty has decreased in Nepal after 1995, income and spending have grown much more uneven. Examining differences between urban and rural regions individually, it is noteworthy that the urban Gini coefficient has stayed almost steady at roughly 0.43. The rural Gini coefficient has climbed from 0.31 to 0.35 throughout the period under consideration. The fact that the total Gini coefficient has grown significantly more than the urban and rural coefficients considered individually implies that the rising difference between urban and rural regions has operated as the most significant equalizing driver in Nepal over the last several decades. Two interconnected factors have been at work here.

First and foremost, urban income, which was already far greater than rural income, has expanded significantly faster than rural income. Because of this, between 1995/96 and 2020, urban per capita expenditure increased at an annual rate of 4.5 percent compared to a rate of 3.5 percent in rural regions, further exacerbating the imbalance between urban and rural spending levels in the country. Second, the urban population has been rising at a far quicker rate than the rural population. In the eight years after 1995, the proportion of people living in urban areas increased by more than 50 percent, from 7 percent to 15 percent. As a result of the fact that urban regions have much greater inequality than rural areas, urbanization has exacerbated general inequality in the traditional pattern. It also contributes to the rise in general inequality in Nepal. There are a variety of factors that contribute to this phenomenon.

First and foremost, increasing inequality in rural Nepal is directly tied to long-standing ethnic imbalances. According to previous research, even though poverty has decreased for all ethnic groups between 1995/96 and 2020, poverty has fallen far more slowly for the lower castes than the rest of society between 1995/96 and 2020/04. This is particularly significant since lower castes already constitute the poorest element of society, and the uneven rate of poverty reduction has already exacerbated severe inequities. Second, increasing inequalities in land ownership have exacerbated the situation. Because these families suffer from far greater poverty levels than bigger landowners, it is reasonable to assume that the movement in population towards the lower end of the land distribution has had an equalizing effect on the distribution of income. Finally, the uneven distribution of remittance money has had a role in the development of the economy. According to survey results, although families of all income levels have seen increases in remittance income between 1995/96 and 2020/04, the wealthier households have had quicker increases in remittance income than the poorer households over the same period. Consider that the per capita remittance income of the wealthiest quintile of families climbed by 150 percent while it increased by just 120 percent among those in the lowest quintile. The health of Nepalese people has improved significantly over the last few decades, thanks to major efforts by the government and the private sector. The gain has been gradual rather than dramatic, and all of the measures have improved in each decade, showing that the underlying mechanisms that have led to the improvement have been rather stable.

Despite continual increases, the absolute levels of most of these indicators continue to be lower than the South Asian average, mostly due to Nepal's starting point in terms of health status being very poor. But what is amazing is that the rate of advancement gained in recent years surpassed the rate of improvement seen by the rest of South Asia at the time. As a result of their strong performance, Nepal and Bangladesh have been standout performers in the region, surpassing the advancement of larger, wealthier nations such as India and Pakistan by a significant margin. Even while the pace of development in education has not been as rapid as that in health, progress has also been achieved in this area. Although there has been significant improvement, it has been considerably more gradual at the secondary level. The gross Enrolment ratio had slowly crept up from 27 percent in early 2017 to just 32 percent in 2018. The general advances achieved on the fronts of health and education, on the other hand, obscure the stark inequities that exist throughout Nepal. Disparities of this kind are seen along ethnic, regional, and gender lines. The lower castes, including the Janajati and Dalits, do far worse than the higher castes, including the Brahmins and Chhetri's, on almost every measure of health and education available.

For example, in recent years, people from the lower castes had an average life expectancy of 50 to 53 years, compared to the Brahmins, who had over 60 years. Similarly, the lower castes had an average of fewer than two years of education, but the higher castes had an average of almost five years of schooling. In addition to racial and ethnic discrepancies, there are also disparities between ecological zones to be considered. The result is that in Nepal's mountains, where most Janajati and Dalits reside, the average life expectancy was just 50 years, compared to a national average of 60 years in the same year. The Far Western and Mid- Western parts of the nation fall behind the rest of the country in terms of health and educational results, per capita income, and general human development. It is no surprise that these are also the locations where the Maoist insurgency has established the most solid footholds.

Chapter 8: Economic Reforms in Nepal

The economy of Nepal saw a significant acceleration in growth during the first half of 2017, but that this acceleration was based on an unsustainable increase of aggregate demand caused by expansionary fiscal and monetary policies during this period. In 2017, public spending grew rapidly, outpacing growth in public income by a corresponding margin, resulting in mounting budget deficits. Particularly notable was the dramatic increase in development expenditure, which rose from 8.7 percent of GDP in the second half of 2017 to 12.4 percent of GDP in the first half of 2018, while government revenue only managed a modest increase, rising from 7.7 percent of GDP to 8.7 percent of GDP during the same period. Consequently, the budget deficit increased by more than double, rising from 3.1 percent of GDP to 6.7 percent of GDP. At the same time, the money supply grew quickly, with the supply of broad money increasing from 16.2 percent of GDP to 27.2 percent.

The implementation of expansionary fiscal and monetary policies did contribute to economic development, which was driven by the non- tradable sectors, particularly construction, in the short term. However, it also rendered the expansion unsustainable by fueling inflation and hurting the balance of trade. For the first time since the beginning of planned development in the 1950s, inflation has maintained consistently in the double digits. According to the Bureau of Labor Statistics, the rate of inflation increased from an average of 7.5 percent in 2017 to an average of 10.6 percent in 2018. The balance of payments position worsened due to the appreciation in the real currency rate in conjunction with growing inflation. Exports fell from 6.0 percent of GDP in the second half of 2017 to 4.9 percent in the first half of 2018, while imports increased from 12.9 percent of GDP to 17 percent over the same period. It harmed the country's trade balance, which deteriorated from 6.9 percent to 12.1 percent of GDP. On the current account balance, it deteriorated from a nearly balanced position to -3 percent. In response to the formation of these macroeconomic imbalances, a stabilization plan was implemented, followed by a structural adjustment program. But the changes did not happen all at once in a furious frenzy, as some had anticipated. Instead, they were stretched out, changing in response to the unfolding events. There are four basic stages of policy change that may be distinguished.

The first reform phase (1985-86) concentrated mostly on typical stabilizing measures, which were largely ineffective. On the contrary, devaluation made matters worse by causing fresh inflation to be triggered. Despite growing inflation, the real exchange rate declined, which assisted in increasing exports. However, imports increased even more rapidly, leading to further deterioration of the current account throughout the second half of 2017. There was little reason for celebration on the budgetary front, as the budget deficit increased slightly from 6.7 percent of GDP in the first half of 2017 to 7.8 percent of GDP. In general, the macroeconomic situation has remained dire for the time being. The second phase, which began in early 1990 and culminated in the election of a democratically elected administration, saw a considerably more serious effort at macroeconomic change than the first phase. During this period, the tax base was enlarged, revenue management was strengthened, and trade and industrial policies were liberalized even more than they were before. A program of gradual tariff reductions was implemented, and quantitative limits were largely eliminated or reduced to nothing. The foreign exchange system was harmonized, and the current account was converted to a convertible currency. Interest rates were liberalized, and more people were able to enter the banking business. The third reform episode began around the year 1997. The deregulation of the agriculture sector, the implementation of a neutral VAT, and the development of local governments were the primary components of the reform. The fourth phase, which began around the year 2000 and lasted until the end of the decade, was more in the character of governance change than macroeconomic reform. The government attempted to enhance tax policy and administration throughout this period, implemented a medium-term spending framework, reorganized the management of Nepal's two major commercial banks, and reinforced financial sector laws and measures to combat corruption. Trade policy was the most significant component of the second wave of reforms launched by the new democratic administration, which aimed to speed the process of trade liberalization while also providing an incentive to exporters via a variety of incentives. Compared to early 2000, average tariff rates had dropped from 32 percent to 14 percent in 2020.

The basic peak tariff has also dropped from 200 to 110 percent, and the number of tariff slabs has decreased from more than 100 in early 2000 to just 5 in 2018. Furthermore, quantitative limitations have been nearly totally removed from the equation. These measures successfully reduced the effective rate of protection in manufacturing from 114 percent in 1989 to 8.5 percent in 1996 as a consequence of their implementation. It is also worth noting that Nepal's number of agricultural tariffs is quite low, ranging between 5 and 25 percent. During the reform process, the exchange rate mechanism was redesigned. In recent years, partial convertibility in the current account was implemented, followed by complete convertibility the following year. The dual exchange rate system that had previously been in place was eliminated, and the exchange rate versus convertible currencies was permitted to be established by the market. However, the official determination of the exchange rate between the Rupee and the currencies of other countries was maintained. Various types of incentives were granted to exporters to offset the export bias of the previous trade system, which was intended to be eliminated.

In addition, measures were made to promote foreign direct investment, with most industries now allowing foreign ownership at 100 percent. Furthermore, foreign investors were permitted to hold up to 25 percent of the shares of publicly traded enterprises. In recent times, a new trade treaty with India was signed, which eliminated the majority of non-tariff trade barriers with India, including the value-added requirement, which required at least 50 percent Nepalese or other countries' raw material content as a condition for receiving duty-free access to the with other country markets. Along with this, investment in Nepal was virtually completely liberalized in comparison to other countries. When taken collectively, these actions represented a significant shift away from the previous system of trade prohibitions. Nepal can presently claim that it has a better degree of openness than most other developing nations in the world. This was shown by the fact that Nepal received a score of two on a scale from zero to ten on the International Monetary Fund's trade restrictiveness index, where a lower number indicates a higher degree of openness. Private sector participation in activities previously reserved for the public sector was a significant component of the second phase of reforms.

8.1 Strategic Reforms for Accelerated Agricultural Growth

The agricultural backwardness of Nepal's economy has long been the country's Achilles' heel. While much of South Asia has increased agricultural output at a higher rate than population growth, defying dire forecasts to the opposite, agricultural development in Nepal has lagged behind population growth by a significant margin. Over the period 1965 to 2020, agricultural GDP increased at a rate of just 2.5 percent per year, slightly higher than the population growth rate of 2.2 percent, while total GDP increased at a pace of 3.8 percent per year. On the one hand, this resulted in a near stasis in per capita agricultural production, while on the other, the proportional contribution of agriculture to total GDP decreased rapidly. Between 2015 and 2020, agriculture's contribution to the nation's gross domestic product decreased from 72 percent to 40 percent. The share of the workers employed in agriculture, on the other hand, did not decrease in the same proportion. A fall in labor productivity in agriculture from more than 90 percent to around 66 percent indicates a secular decline in agricultural labor productivity, which has remained a severe hindrance to Nepal's potential to accelerate economic development and alleviate poverty over the long term. The low level of input consumption and the continuous dependence on archaic technologies are the primary causes of poor productivity development. For example, just 40 percent of farmland in Nepal was irrigated by 2019, even though two-thirds of the country's total cultivable territory is theoretically irrigable, and only

17 percent of that land got year-round irrigation. Part of the difficulty stems from Nepal's harsh and hilly topography, making it difficult to expand irrigation at a reasonable cost due to its remoteness. Thus, more than two-thirds of irrigated land is located in Terai's plain topography, with just 16 percent being in the hills. However, even in the Terai, year-round irrigation is confined to about 20 percent of the area, much less than the potential. Furthermore, the facilities that are now in place are not adequately maintained.

It has been estimated that cost recovery rates for government-managed irrigation systems, which account for the vast majority of Nepal's irrigation system, are somewhat more than one percent (World Bank, 2005a). Even though systems run by participatory water user groups have a far better track record in cost recovery and maintenance, this does not completely fix the issue since the government must be engaged in large-scale projects. According to the data obtained by the Nepal Living Standards Surveys in 2020/04, just around 5 percent of agricultural families used improved types of seeds. According to the same report, about a third of farmers do not use any organic fertilizers at all, and even those who do use them do so at quantities well below the recommended limits. It is estimated that most farmers have very limited access to financing via the official banking system. A total of 14 percent of families have access to credit, with just 8 percent of households in the poorest quintile able to get it. One of the fundamental structural difficulties underpinning Nepal's agricultural economy is the vast disparity in access to land between the rich and the poor. More than two-thirds of families own less than one hectare of land, accounting for just around 30 percent of all farmlands in the country. In comparison, just 1.5 percent of holdings possess plots larger than 5 hectares and account for only 14 percent of all cultivated land in the country. Approximately 16 percent of rural families are landless in the strictest sense.

The Land Reform Act of 1962 set ownership limits and tenancy rights for the first time. However, the redistributive goal of the Act was only partially achieved, with just 1.5 percent of the land being transferred under it. Consequently, the great majority of farmers continue to have insufficient control over their property, which hurts both their motivation and capacity to implement productivity-enhancing measures. Nepal has a long history of using a dual tenure system, which enabled both landlords and tenants to claim land ownership. Both claimants were discouraged from investing in land due to the system of split property rights in place at the time of the settlement. Dual ownership was abolished, and the property was physically divided between the landlord and the tenant under the terms of a 1995 Land Act amendment that attempted to resolve the situation. However, the law's execution has been virtually ineffective. Another structural concern is the geographical isolation of many agricultural settlements in the hills and mountains, which are not linked to modern infrastructure, exacerbating the difficulty in obtaining inputs and selling their produce at competitive prices. The Nepal Living Standards Survey conducted in 1995/96 discovered, for example, that chemical and fertilizer inputs are seldom utilized if a farmer lives more than five hours away from the closest market. Furthermore, more profitable vegetable cultivation occurs within three hours' driving distance of a major urban market. In comparison, subsistence farming of grains and pulses predominates in regions within eight hours' driving distance of a major urban market in general. The local economy is self-sufficient when traveling more than eight hours, with minimal engagement with the outside world. Agricultural progress in Nepal has been stifled due to a combination of factors The result may be seen in that, between the early 1960s and late 2020, paddy yields increased at a rate of barely

0.6 percent per year, whereas yields in neighboring nations increased at rates ranging between 1.4 and 2 percent per year. The Nepalese government implemented a thorough program of agricultural reforms as part of the larger economic reforms implemented throughout that decade to address the deep-seated structural difficulties in the country's agricultural sector. The reform was executed in two stages: first, it was approved and then implemented. Initial improvements were bundled as part of the Agricultural Perspective Plan (APP), introduced in 1995 as part of the Ninth Plan, and implemented over five years. A regionally balanced agricultural development strategy was proposed in the Plan, with the dual aim of increasing efficiency via specialization following regional comparative advantage and guaranteeing that the impoverished people of all areas may benefit from the growing process. The idea of this strategy was to pursue two distinct sets of policies for Nepal's two major ecological zones – namely, the Terai plains and the hills and mountains– to address the needs of each region. When it came to food production, the Terai was to be targeted for the production of staple foods, while the hills and mountains were to be targeted for the promotion of livestock and higher-valued commercial crops, and the two regions were to grow in a complementary manner by creating demand for one another.

While the Perspective Plan was largely executed in reality, the second phase of reforms, tied to an Asian Development Bank loan signed and financed by the Second Agricultural Program Loan, quickly surpassed the first phase of reforms. While the new set of reforms continued to promote the differentiated development, strategy based on regional comparative advantage, it signified a significant move away from government intervention as the major instrument of growth in favor of market liberalization as the primary instrument of growth. The government's monopoly on the import and distribution of critical commodities like fertilizer and irrigation equipment has been lifted, allowing for more private sector engagement in the distribution chain overall. While this was going on, fertilizer and irrigation equipment prices were deregulated at the retail level, and subsidies were phased out, except a tiny amount of transportation subsidy to stimulate the flow of inputs into distant regions. It was possible to achieve this improvement via the increasing use of modern inputs, greater cropping intensity, and diversification into higher- value crops. Despite these beneficial advances, there has been some debate regarding how much credit should be given to the reforms as a whole.

The first point to mention is that any attempt to evaluate the effects of reforms by comparing performance is somewhat problematic because agriculture experienced unusually low growth in the first half of the decade. It could be argued that all that happened in the second half was that the growth rate returned to the levels experienced in 2017. To begin with, any examination of increased performance must consider the fact that, in addition to agricultural changes, there were other factors at work within the economy that may account for at least some of the improvement. In particular, the substantial growth in the flow of remittances and the signing of a relatively liberal trade treaty with India in 1996 were two of the most significant of these developments. It is debatable how significant these demand-side pressures were compared to the effects of changes working on the supply-side in the long run. There are legitimate concerns about whether or not the supply-side incentives have improved at all due to the revisions.

Among other things, in the second half of the decade, agriculture's inter-sectoral terms of trade decreased compared to the first half. There are also some signs that the privatization of input distribution and the elimination of subsidies may have made it more difficult for small farmers in distant locations to get vital supplies like fertilizer. All of this directly impacted crop yield and profitability, which were both reduced as a result of the situation. According to survey data, the yield of field crops per hectare decreased by 7 percent between 1995/96 and 2000/04, while the cost of production per hectare grew by 46 percent over the same period.

8.2 Current Programs and the Nepal Poverty Alleviation Fund

The government of Nepal, like many other nations in the area, has adopted a wide variety of targeted interventions aimed at improving the lives of certain categories of poor and disadvantaged people. Three types of programmers may be distinguished: those that are aimed at particular places, those that are focused on certain demographic groups, and those that use a specific entry point (for example, credit) to reach their intended beneficiaries. Despite considerable overlap among these categories, this categorization offers a useful framework for understanding the wide range of targeted interventions that have been implemented in Nepal. In areas that have been recognized as being significantly more backward, rural, isolated, and endowed with a lesser degree of socio- economic infrastructure, area-based programmers have been launched to address these issues. This kind of initiative includes the Remote Area

Development Programmed (RADP) and is one of the most significant.

By late 2020, this initiative had expanded to include twenty-two districts, with a strong focus on constructing transportation infrastructure and other infrastructure. There were additional provisions for skill development, women's training, and training in horticulture and vegetable cultivation, among other things. This initiative was intended to complement the decentralization process, which the Nepalese government was attempting to revitalize at the same time as this one. As a result, the resources for this program were assigned and dispersed to the individual Village Development Committees (VDCs) by the central government office. People at the grassroots level, on the other hand, were either absent or had little interest in participating. The Special Area Development Programme (SADP) was established as a political reaction to people's outpouring of dissatisfaction and disgust with prolonged economic misery. In certain regions, it manifested itself in violent eruptions of rage. Following the application of criteria such as backwardness, remoteness, poor levels of socio-economic infrastructure, and the presence of current Maoist operations, twenty-five districts were chosen, of which twenty- two were previously included in the RADP. RADP had a narrower emphasis than this program, which attempted to encourage agricultural and livestock and infrastructure development in addition to infrastructure development.

The target-group-focused programmers have been created, with a particular emphasis on indigenous people, untouchables (Dalits), so- called socially and economically disadvantaged groups (SEDG), women, and children, among other groups. Specific efforts taken by the first two groups have included reserving a portion of the government's funding for Village Development Committees (VDCs) and social mobilization with the assistance of non-governmental organizations (NGOs). Groups classified as Socially and Economically Disadvantaged (SEDG) include bonded laborers, migrant household, marginal farmers and landless

124 Why Nepal Fails

peasants, disabled people, senior citizens, and members of certain backward ethnic groups who do not fall under the specific classification. The Kamaiya Debt Relief Program and the Kamaiya Skill Training Program for bonded laborers, land resettlement projects for Sucumbíos and landless/marginal peasants, and different safety nets programme for older citizens widows and disabled individuals are among the programme available to this population. The majority of these programs, on the other hand, are of limited scope, and nothing is known about their effectiveness. A National Plan of Action for Women was launched in 1981, marking the beginning of Nepal's Sixth Five-Year Plan. It was the first time those specific policies and programs for women were implemented. From a long-term viewpoint, the most significant measure performed so far has been the provision of scholarships to female college and university students. Other initiatives have tried to improve the economic standing of women. The Women Farmers Programmed, Production Credit for Rural Women (PCRW), and Micro Credit Project for Women are just a few of the programs run by the Ministry of Local Development, which also includes credit provided by five regional banks, Grameen-Bank type replications as well as Community Development Programs run by non-governmental organizations (MCPW). Several of these programs overlap with entry-point-based interventions. The entrance-point-based program has used three primary entry points – namely, credit, institution, and infrastructure – to access the program. Since the Small Farmer's Development Programmed (SFDP) in 2015, credit-based programs have played an important role in Nepal's economic development. Small farmers (defined as individuals who owned less than 1 hectare of land in the hills and 2.67 hectares of land in the Terai were provided with credit via group organizations and in the form of collateral-free loans to support their productive activities. Because the overarching focus of a later reinvigorated SFDP was to create local institutional capacity to build self- sustaining credit-providing institutions at the local level.

Several programs, such as the Production Credit for Rural Women (PCRW) and the Micro Credit Project for Women was designed in the same vein as the SFPD but explicitly aimed at women (MCPW). The Partnership for Rural Women (PCRW) was established in 1982 to enhance the income of underprivileged rural women via the provision of loans and other services. By late 2020, it had been adopted in 67 districts throughout Nepal. The effect of PCRW on rural women has been overwhelmingly favorable in terms of their empowerment and the development of their self-reliance and consciousness. MCPW was established in 1994 with a similar goal to that of PCRW but with two significant variances. Women from low-income urban and rural families were among the intended beneficiaries of the project, which sought to offer finance and other services via the employment of non-governmental organizations (NGOs) as intermediaries. As of October 2020, a total of 88 non-governmental organizations (NGOs) had been recruited and educated for this purpose.

According to an internal progress chapter issued by the Ministry of Local Government, the program is distinguished by a very high debt recovery rate – as high as 98 percent in certain cases. The establishment by Nepal Rastra Bank of five regional rural development banks (RRDB) as a replication of the Grameen Bank model of Bangladesh, the Banking with the Poor Program, which was launched by Rastriya Banijya Bank, and the Rural Micro-Credit Development Centre (RMDC), which was established with the responsibility of providing wholesale credit to poor people through a variety of intermediary organizations. The targeted lending programs have benefited many women and men in rural regions, enabling them to generate more income and expand their employment.

On the other hand, many of these programs have suffered from mistargeting, a lack of knowledge of poor people's absorptive capacity, a deteriorating repayment percentage, high service delivery costs, a lack of local institutional capacity, and an inability to retain qualified employees. Others have suffered due to a lack of support services, such as technology, extension services, market access, and so on. In particular, programmed focused on people facing extreme poverty, such as the Kamaiya's, for whom comprehensive support services in the form of a comprehensive package were vital, have suffered as a result. To address poverty alleviation at the local level, institution- based programs have concentrated on increasing institutional capacity, promoting decentralization, and strengthening local government. This is the first program in Nepal, having been established in 2015 as part of the Small Farmers Development Program. Its primary emphasis was on developing groups at the local level for load distribution and additional services. It emerged that the main challenge in the early stages of its implementation was the insufficient quality of group creation, as most of the groups lacked proper training and experience, resulting in poor loan management, low loan recovery, and other issues. Intending to develop the institutional management capacities of small farmer organizations, the Small Farmer Development Program (SFDP) has progressively embraced the idea of Institutional Development Programmed (IDP) to overcome this deficiency. The Small Farmers' Cooperative Limited (SFCL) was established in 1987/88 as an experimental project using this innovative idea. The SFCL quickly spread across the nation and became a model for other cooperatives. When comparing the performance of SFCL to that of the SFDP, it was discovered that the payback rate was higher, the administrative costs were lower, and the density of coverage and mobilization of local resources were larger.

From previous years to the present, two important projects in the field of targeted interventions have been undertaken. The initial attempt was founded on the awareness that previous programs and policies had failed to address the basic issues of social exclusion that many different demographic groups were facing at the time. Women made up half of the population, individuals living in the Western to the far Western Hills made up 22 percent of the population and served as a hotspot for Maoist insurrection, untouchables (Dalits), and indigenous people who made up 46 percent of the population. Because the government of Nepal has recognized that the roots of injustices that lead to social exclusion run deep in the country's culture, it has lately undertaken a bold endeavor to move beyond standard poverty alleviation programs and engage in a variety of positive activities. In recent years, there has been a flurry of landmark legislation designed to mitigate or remove existing restrictive laws, such as revisions to the Civil Code (Inheritance Law and Property Bill) in recent year, which granted women the right to inherit and hold the property for the first time in Nepal's history, and affirmative action programs and policies designed to ensure greater representation of women and caste/ethnic groups in civil society organizations, such as the Nepal Women's Association.

The National Foundation for the Development of Indigenous Nationalities (NFDIN) was established by legislation in 2019 to enhance the well-being of Janajati people across the country[87]. In addition to general programmers, it has implemented various unique initiatives, such as the Cheeping Development Program and special scholarship programmers for impoverished Ganapati communities. In a similar vein, the National Dalit Commission was founded by executive order in 2019 to serve the interests of the untouchables in the country. Dalit students have been the exclusive beneficiaries of national scholarships, which have allowed them to pursue studies at all levels, from basic to higher education. Additionally, sixty-five income and skill-oriented programmers were in place to improve the living conditions of Dalit families. The second significant step was the establishment of the Poverty Alleviation Fund (PAF), which became operational in recent years.

Created with cooperation from external partners and government resources, the PAF is intended to serve as an umbrella organization for all

---

87 Indigenous Peoples of Nepal. https://english.indigenousvoice.com/indigenous-peoples-of- nepal

types of targeted programmers, including affirmative action programmers, to combat social exclusion and other forms of discrimination. The primary goal is to enhance the lives of rural poor and socially excluded people by establishing infrastructure, employment, and income-generating possibilities in the country's most depressed villages and communities. The activities that will be carried out with the help of this Fund are anticipated to be demand-driven, with NGOs and community-based organizations (CBOs) acting as support groups. Community subprojects will be carried out primarily via the efforts of partner groups (POs). These POs may be DDCs, VDCs, local NGOs, or private sector organizations. Still, they would all need to establish a track record of engaging with the target people in their communities and earning their confidence. As part of their responsibilities, POs will help communities prepare subproject proposals and submit those proposals to PAF. They will also monitor the quality of participation and connect with government agencies and other programmers. Beneficiaries would need to organize themselves to get benefits from PAF. The subprojects may, for example, assist existing community organizations, self-help groups, forest user groups, water user groups, and other groups founded around economic activities that are already active. Unfortunately, the functioning of the PAF has been severely impeded, as has been the case with the majority of other undertakings in Nepal, by the Maoist insurgency and the ongoing political instability. Following on from the previous debate, it is obvious that Nepal has had the chance to experiment with a wide range of targeted interventions for the poor.

On the other hand, independent studies have shown that most of them have failed to fulfill their declared objectives over an extended period. Small Farmers' Development Programme (SFDP), Production Credit for Rural Women (PCRW), and Micro Credit Project for Women are just a few of the success stories (MCPW). The endeavor to establish institutions that underlay each seems to have been the key to their success. Institutions that have made it possible for beneficiaries to engage at all stages of programmed implementation, in particular, contributed to the success of the initiative. In this setting, the initiatives at decentralization that have been attempted from time to time have a unique significance. Various types of decentralization have been practiced in Nepal for a long time. Still, they were mostly employed to suit the interests of the governing elites at the center of the country. Following the constitutional changes of 2018, attempts at genuine decentralization were made, first with the Local Body (LB) Acts and then with the landmark Local Self Governance Act (LSGA, the principles of which were subsequently incorporated into the Ninth and Tenth Plans of the United Nations. For decentralization to effectively assist the poor, it was understood that people needed to be empowered at the grassroots level. This empowerment could only be achieved by the mobilization of individuals and groups into autonomous community organizations. The United Nations Development Program (UNDP) provided significant impetus in this respect, conceptualizing and implementing programmers such as the Participatory District Development Programmed (PDDP) and the Local Governance Program (LGP).

As part of fiscal decentralization, the government started granting development funds to local governments to support the implementation of local development initiatives and the development of their institutional capacity at the same time. Local governments took over several government functions, including elementary and secondary education, primary and basic health care, agricultural extension, and livestock services. Furthermore, the provision of small-scale drinking water and irrigation facilities, the building of agricultural roads, and the maintenance of district and urban highways were delegated to the local authorities. The decentralization process has been hampered by internal uncertainty and challenges inherent in the decentralization process, despite the government's efforts. Damage or destruction of physical infrastructure caused by the Maoist insurgency severely hampered the capacity of local authorities to operate properly. Parallel to that, the political tug of war that raged for many years between the king and opposition parties and Maoists on the other resulted in the absence of elected members in the local bodies for numerous years. Instead of elected representatives, local-level government employees assumed the tasks delegated to local organizations; a significant step backward from the participatory decentralization that Nepal had pioneered which was widely praised at the time.

Chapter 9: The Political Environment in Nepal

Nepal's internal politics have been through a tumultuous and major transformation in recent years. In response to the request of Prime Minister KP Sharma Oli, President Bidya Devi Bhandari dissolved the House of Representatives[88], and called for quick elections in April and May of the following year. A significant internal division within the governing Nepal Communist Party (NCP) had threatened to remove Oli, prompting him to take the unprecedented step. The action has been denounced as unlawful by opposition parties and other civil society organizations. Many writs have been filed against it at the Supreme Court (SC), continuing proceedings. Massive demonstrations have taken place around the country in opposition to the prime minister's decision. If the Supreme Court reinstates the parliament, Oli is on the verge of losing his moral authority to rule and might be subjected to a no-confidence vote in his administration. If the Supreme Court upholds his decision, it is uncertain if he would retake control of the government with a majority. It was thought that the establishment of a strong administration in Nepal after decades of political turmoil would result in a significant socioeconomic change. Regardless of the Supreme Court's judgment, political tensions

---

88 Political Instability and Uncertainty Loom Large in Nepal.
https://southasianvoices.org/politi- cal-instability-and-uncertainty-in-nepal/

in the nation are certain to worsen in the coming days. A serious and long-term weakening of Nepal's democratic fabric will result from the internal rift that resulted in the dissolution of parliament in December, as well as the political dimensions of the current predicament and the domestic and geopolitical ramifications of internal political instability.

As a result of the differences between NCP Chair Oli and former Prime Minister Pushpa Kamal Dahal, the party has become more vertically divided. The former is the most extreme. A coalition of the Oli-led Communist Party of Nepal Unified Marxist Leninist (UML) and the Dahal-led Communist Party of Nepal (Maoist Center or MC) won almost two-thirds of the seats in the country's legislative elections. The two parties combined to become the National Coalition Party (NCP). Internal politics, on the other hand, undermined this union. Even though both groups claim to be representatives of the real party, the Election Commission has requested explanations from both factions before deciding on the topic. A group that can support its claim by producing the signatures of at least 40 percent of its central committee members is qualified to be recognized as the official party, according to Section 5.1 of the Political Party Act. The group that has been formally acknowledged will be allowed to keep the party name and election symbol. In contrast, the faction that has not been officially recognized will be required to register as a new party, jeopardizing its future electoral chances.

A group headed by Dahal, and former Prime Minister Madhav Kumar Nepal was preparing to launch a no-confidence vote against Oli. Still, Oli, seeing an immediate danger to his position, opted to move for the dissolution of the parliament rather than risk losing his position. Several internal political dynamics inside the NCP have contributed to the present level of turbulence within the party. He claims that Oli has violated the power-sharing agreement reached the founding of NCP, which stated that he was obliged to pass up either the premiership or the executive chairmanship to Dahal if he did not agree to do so. After reaching an agreement, Oli and Dahal agreed that Oli would balance his tenure as prime minister and Dahal would serve as the party's executive chair. On the other hand, Oli has shown no indication that he intends to step down from either position, raising tensions inside the party.

Additionally, Oli made unilateral selections to several cabinet and government posts, further solidifying his influence over the newly established National Coalition Party (NCP). He also marginalized Madhav Kumar Nepal, a prominent leader of the Nepal Communist Party and a former prime minister, prompting Nepal to support Dahal against Oli. As a result, Oli opted to dissolve parliament and seek a new mandate rather than face a no-confidence vote in his government. It is important to note that the party unity between the Unified Marxist Leninist (CPN- UML) and the Maoist CPN (MC) did not result in the envisioned doctrinal oneness. Geopolitical issues and foreign players have always influenced Nepal's internal political scene. To strengthen his grip on the NCP, Oli has recently attempted to improve relations with India, which have been strained due to Nepal's inclusion of disputed territories in its new political map. As a result, high-level delegations from both countries have visited Nepal recently. As part of its vaccine diplomacy efforts in the area, India has also given Nepal one million doses of the COVID-19 vaccine, developed in collaboration with the United States. While India has intervened in Nepal's domestic politics in the past, it has framed the present power struggle as an "internal problem" to avoid a reaction from Nepali policymakers and avert a possible spread of political turmoil in the country. However, in recent years, China's ascension in Nepal has posed a serious threat to India's historically dominating position.

China believes Nepal to be critical to its national security policy because of concerns that Tibetans may use Nepali territory to undertake anti-Chinese operations on the country's land. Beijing has generally had a non-interventionist approach to foreign policy; however, this stance is increasingly changing, as seen by the aggressive attempts of the Chinese ambassador to Nepal to solve current difficulties inside the Nepal Communist Party (NCP). Because of the ideological connection between the NCP and the Communist Party of China, Nepal's media speculates that China favors preserving the NCP's existence, believing that this would allow China to exercise more political and economic influence over Nepal. Even though China is well aware of India's long-standing influence in Nepal, the country is wary of growing American interest in the Himalayan nation. This is especially true in light of Oli's efforts to get the United States Millennium Challenge Corporation (MCC) grant assistance to construct electrical transmission lines in the Himalayan nation approved by the country's parliament.

On the other hand, Dahal has expressed opposition to the MCC and has labeled it as a component of the United States-led Indo-Pacific Strategy to control China. Given that Nepal is a signatory to China's Belt and Road Initiative, Beijing may favor development projects that are conducted inside the BRI framework and may pressure the Nepali government to postpone or reject projects led by the United States. Political stability in Nepal was supposed to bring about economic prosperity after the political reforms that ended the country's decade-long military struggle. Furthermore, under Oli's leadership, a strong majority government boosted prospects for the achievement of modernization. Unfortunately, the governing party leaders have instead been embroiled in a fierce power struggle, and corruption scandals in the government have eroded public confidence in the administration.

Nepali Congress (NC) is the largest opposition party in Nepal, and it is seeking a split in the ruling Nepal Communist Party (NCP-UML) to increase its chances of winning power in the future. The NC has condemned Oli's call for hasty elections as illegal. Still, it has also declared that it will not oppose polls if the Supreme Court chooses to dissolve the lower chamber of the parliament in the future. Recognizing the growing instability in the country, several royalist parties and groups have accused the government of corruption and demonstrated on the streets, calling for the restoration of the Hindu state and constitutional monarchy to reinvent and stabilize Nepal's image and national identity.

The NCP was given a five-year mandate to rule the nation by the people in the recent legislative elections. On the other hand, Oli chose to seek a new mandate, arguing that the Dahal-Nepal group was interfering with the government's ability to operate properly. Because of an internal personality divide within the party, domestic political instability has unfortunately emerged due to the party's resurgence. This deteriorating democratic scenario will not benefit either India or China, both of which are concerned about possible spillover consequences. Even if the Supreme Court upholds Oli's decision, elections in April are not certain. A constitutional crisis might erupt if elections are not conducted within six months of the date of the dissolution of the legislature. If the Supreme Court overturns Oli's judgment, he might be forced to resign as prime minister and leader of the National Congress Party. Nepali politics is expected to be characterized by increasing insecurity in the coming months regardless of the result. In recent times, Supreme court has ordered president to appoint Congress leader Deuba as prime minister of Nepal. The supreme court stated that decision to dissolve parliament was unlawful and appointment of Deuba as the next Prime minister of Nepal citing article 76(5) of the Constitution of Nepal[89].

9.1 Political Uncertainty Hurts Nepal's Economy

Anil Shah, the CEO of Nabil Bank, one of Nepal's major commercial banks, authored an opinion piece for the Himalaya Post. He put forth five pillars of sustainable economic growth for the country. Shah emphasized the need for political stability as a prerequisite for the long-term success of each of the five pillars of progress. But even while he was writing, Nepal's MPs were arguing whether to extend the term of the Constituent

---

89 https://www.reuters.com/world/asia-pacific/nepals-supreme-court-reinstates-parliament-or- ders-new-pm-be-appointed-2021-07-12/

Assembly beyond May 28, which would result in a further delay in the proclamation of a new constitution. The debate continues today. It's the second time they've done so in as many years. As of 2015, Nepal is still mired in the same political stalemate that it has been in previous years, when political groups decided to end a decades-old civil conflict. With a query, Shah concluded his op-ed piece: "Will political stability gives way to economic change, or will economic change give way to political stability?" he wondered. The nation's economy remains stagnant as foreign and local investors wait for evidence of political stability before making a decision. Businesses, banks, and ordinary residents are all unable to go forward while one political impasse after another develops.

According to the Nepal Stock Exchange (NEPSE), the index stood at 413.98 on May 9, down nearly 18 percent from the same date last year. Bank profits have slowed as people lose confidence in the banking system. A liquidity crunch develops as interest rates rise, even as the real estate sector experiences a sharp decline. Recently, when asked about Nepal's financial sector by a local news outlet, Ashoke SJB Rana, CEO of Himalayan Bank Ltd and newly elected president of the Nepal Bankers' Association, pointed out that investors have been putting their money into real estate while staying away from riskier, but more productive ventures, such as development projects and tourism as well as health and education. And, even though 2020 has been designated as Nepal Tourism Year (with the government setting an ambitious goal of attracting one million tourists to the country in 2020), a Maoist trade union protesting the dismissal of a hotel employee took over a well-known resort lodge in Pokhara, one of the country's most popular tourist destinations, forcing the hotel to relocate all one hundred and twenty of its guests to other hotels throughout the city. Since the beginning of 2015, Nepal has been experiencing political instability, resulting in an atmosphere of uncertainty, which has dampened business activity and the macroeconomic climate across the nation.

This uncertainty permeates not just the national attitude but also the sub-national level, as shown by the fact that the Nepal approximately five dozen small and large companies located in the Industrial Corridor region in the Parsa district have been shuttered for the last two years as a result of labor conflicts, resulting in the loss of employment on a scale of twenty thousand. According to the Chamber of Commerce and Industry, large enterprises such as Annapurna Textile, Puja Soap and Chemical, and Okhati Soap remained closed throughout this period. According to the consensus, the local authorities responsible for reopening the shuttered enterprises have failed to do so. The combination of rising unemployment and workers' dissatisfaction with their government's leadership has contributed to the perpetuation of a cycle of social tension and instability. At the same time, there are glimmering rays of optimism that Nepal may not only be in control of the brakes, but it might also hold the keys to its future prosperity. We had the opportunity to participate in a public-private discussion (PPD) conducted by The Asia Foundation earlier this month in the same city of Pokhara. PPDs are a valuable method for assisting in the implementation of suitable regulatory changes as well as the removal of barriers to private sector investment and development. In particular, small and medium-sized firms (MSMEs) are among the most important engines of sustainable economic development in Nepal, offering job opportunities, technical innovation, flexibility, and competitiveness to the wider economy. When their potential to expand is limited by limitations in the business environment, economic development, market efficiency, and poverty reduction initiatives are all harmed. PPDs provide forums for key stakeholders, including local entrepreneurs and other private sector actors, local business associations and Chambers of Commerce, civil society organizations, and government officials, to come together and form reform coalitions – often in places where none or only inadequate forums currently exist.

In Pokhara, they were engaged in just the same activity. An issue was raised by the president of a local community fisheries association, , about how to proceed with a planned investment in the production of small fish fry (a term used in the fish farming industry to refer baby fish), which can be nurtured and grown for sale at the local fish market. The National Fisheries Research Centre handles current fish fry production in Pokhara. Still, if the local fishery association were to receive adequate training and access to financing to purchase land along with a lake and aquaculture equipment, the local association would be able to take over the business and free up the Research Center's resources to pursue other endeavors. Nepal imports 90   percent of larger-grown fish and pays a premium for   the privilege of doing so.

The Association of Few Fishermen, for example, believes that if local anglers, rather than the government, take up this effort and raise domestic output while simultaneously cutting the price of fish, it would be a win- win situation for both fishermen and customers in Nepal. In reality, this is something that the fisherman has been thinking about for quite some time. The trouble was that they lacked the necessary tools to deal with it. In addition, they had no idea what resources were available to help them, who to contact to receive information on access to financing, what lands were available, or at what price they may be able to purchase them. The PPD process provided them with a venue to bring all of the stakeholders together at one table – the District Development Committee, the District Agricultural Development Officer, scientists from the Research Center, and the local branch of a microfinance bank – and gather all of the information at the same time, which was extremely beneficial. More steps must be taken before the fishermen can achieve their objective of producing their fish fry. Still, these discussions have provided them with an excellent starting point, demonstrating that hurdles can be overcome, and positive change can occur in the fishing industry.

9.2 Effects of Political Instability

With the restoration of multi-party democracy, the expectations and ambitions of Nepal's citizens for a free and wealthy country were deep. The emotion was understandable, given that the framework they envisioned ensured that everyone, even those who did not belong to the top class, had an equal chance at success. The unfortunate reality is that, after three decades of democracy, their expectations and vision have not been realized yet. In the previous thirty-one years, the nation has had twenty-eight different administrations, all of which have been held captive by petty party politics, preventing any substantial developmental progress. Nepal established federalism, reinvigorating hopes for economic success and attempting to resolve the plethora of difficulties that have arisen due to ethnic groups' years of non-participation in the political process. A two-thirds majority administration in the country's Parliament signaled the beginning of an era of political stability.

However, the continuation of political chaos has diverted attention away from strengthening federalism and subscribing to the economic development objective of establishing an enabling environment for entrepreneurship and investment to achieve sustainable economic growth. One might even argue that, except for a few parties, federalism was never the primary objective of political parties in Nepal. Many federal nations, both old and young, have adopted the concept of market-preserving federalism. However, the establishment of Nepal's federal system seems to have been a sudden event, with little or no internalization of concepts among the country's major political parties. Nepal has also seen a contraction in its economic, political, and civic spaces as time has progressed. Many Nepalese are taken aback by the fact that such shrinking of economic, political, and civil spaces has occurred at the hands of those who were once their defenders and the most outspoken critics of any infringement of civil and political rights at the hands of the monarchy[90].

The current government has registered bills that restrict media freedom, artists have been detained on defamation charges, and a mockery of the

---

90 Nepal: Political instability, growth, and the role of think-tanks.
   https://www.freiheit.org/south- asia/nepal-political-instability-growth-and-role-think-
   tanks

federal system has been made (with then-Prime Minister KP Sharma Oli going so far as to say, "Provinces are the administrative units of the federal government")[91]. Appointments to constitutional bodies have been made with complete disregard for due process, and, most significantly, the House of Representatives has been dissolved without a vote. Conflicts between political parties have served neither the governing nor opposition parties' interests. One might even say that the present political turbulence in which we find ourselves is a consequence of disagreements between the political leadership of the various parties. There is some comfort in knowing that one may still turn to the courts for help, even in these trying times. In contrast, even a robust and durable judicial system cannot make up for a weak and ineffective executive branch. A new prime minister who has the support of the House of Representatives is in place in Nepal; however, cabinet seats have yet to be filled, and the government has yet to take form. The selection of Umesh Shrestha as State Minister for Health has been contentious, with analysts claiming that Shrestha is unqualified for the post due to obvious conflicts of interest stemming from his ownership and involvement in some companies in the health and education sectors.

It is conceivable that ministerial posts will be utilized as negotiating chips in the coming days if they have not already been exploited in this manner. It has been made abundantly clear by the recent political turbulence, which has seen two House dissolutions and resulted in a change of government as a result of Supreme Court intervention, that the common vision of the people is not secondary to political advantages of their leaders. According to the average Nepalese citizen, Nepali politics has fragmented, and that the country is once again struggling to uphold democratic norms. The long-running efforts to straighten up politics have come at a tremendous cost. The fact that Nepal has managed to

---

91   Nepal: Political instability, growth, and the role of think-tanks.
    https://www.freiheit.org/south- asia/nepal-political-instability-growth-and-role-of-think-
    tanks

accomplish a few positives in the social spectrum is undeniable. The significance of the lost three decades, on the other hand, is most obvious in the economic sector of the country. The majority of Nepalese are still struggling to fulfill even their most basic requirements, with more than a third of the population in danger of sliding into absolute poverty due to this. As a result of the severe political and economic turbulence, voters are becoming more skeptical of their political and economic leaders.

Thousands of young people have fled to nations with many economic prospects to secure a brighter future. Given the growth of such negative emotions, Nepal's future is almost certain to be grim in the foreseeable future. Now more than ever, it is important for Nepal to successfully implement federalism to avoid further deterioration of the national view. This would be a critical step towards making amends for errors made in the past and chances squandered. Strengthening federalism and ensuring political stability would allow Nepal to concentrate on economic growth, allowing Nepalese citizens to take advantage of the numerous opportunities that would be made available to them as a result of this development, knowing that they would each receive a fair share of the fruits of their labor, allowing them to live a prosperous life in the process. In the next years, civil society groups will play an increasingly important role in aiding the government, particularly sub-national governments confronted with a huge information gap. As a first step, civil society organizations (CSOs) and think tanks should make better use of the resources at their disposal for a more robust discussion on Nepali democracy and the concepts of limited government about preserving the spirit of the constitution. A culture of holding leaders responsible concerning their pledges and manifestos is necessary to institutionalize liberal democracy. This culture can only be established via a greater political dialogue. Consequently, civil society organizations and think tanks must develop into dynamic institutions that grow and maintain conversation and discourse.

The majority of the conversation and discourse should be backed up by research and policy proposals. Again, the importance of civil society organizations (CSOs) and think tanks in this area cannot be overstated and may even be larger than before. But, perhaps most importantly, civil society organizations and think tanks are well-positioned to close the knowledge gap in sub-national governments, especially in provincial administrations. Because the Constitution of Nepal delegated some critical tasks to provincial governments, and because there is a clear lack of ability in the provinces, think tanks and civil society organizations (CSOs) must use this opportunity without delay. On a more positive note, we are already witnessing several think-tanks and civil society organizations (CSOs) closely collaborating with provincial governments on a wide range of issues; however, the engagement is nowhere near sufficient to close the knowledge gap, and, as a result, additional engagement will be required. Overall, utilizing the knowledge and capacity of think tanks will not only assist in the creation of an environment conducive to much- needed political stability and economic growth in Nepal, but it will also contribute to the preservation of the nation's democratic ideals and, most importantly, the preservation of the federal structure itself.

9.3 Why Do Politics Fail in Nepal?

A recent article written by Chandra Ghimire in Kathmandu Post stated that Nepal is becoming a nation of failed policies to the point that it is now a suitable testing ground for actual instances of failed policies92. Why does a nation repeatedly suffer embarrassing policy implementation failures? One can employ a framework made up of a number of success elements taken from PA Brynard's writings in order to come up with an accurate response. The execution of a policy may be examined based on the synthesized works to map the contributing components and estimate the degree of their impacts.

---

92 https://kathmandupost.com/columns/2022/02/10/why-policies-fail-in-nepal

According to Brynard's thesis, a policymaker must coordinate 18 aspects in order to succeed in their endeavors. Depending on the nation and civilization, the factors may play a different function. The practical approach to decision-making comes first and foremost. You must have a distinct vision and a methodical procedure that is supported by solid research. The team's upbeat outlook is the second. This emphasizes the necessity of all policy team members having a positive, team-oriented, and persistent attitude. Third, the capacity of policy bodies to be implemented depends on the dedication of policy leaders. The degree of political and administrative will demonstrated by this is significant. Stakeholder behavior that is cooperative and collaborative comes in fourth. It encourages strong coordination among all stakeholders.

Effective planning, which enables detailed activity organization, is the sixth factor. The sixth variable is how well human resources are mobilized. This enables the greatest use of qualified and driven human resources. Seventh, inspiring excitement is constantly a crucial factor in the implementation of effective policies. Employees are energized and constantly driven by the element of excitement. The eighth aspect that gives a policy a strong foundation for rapid adoption is leadership. This gives them the power to command, the vision to lead, and the authority to advance. The position of political responsibility, in the ninth place, continues to have an impact on the success or failure of a policy. The politician who holds the post eventually has the most power and is in the driver's seat.

The leadership team members' management style is the tenth component of the framework, and its effectiveness depends on how much excitement and optimism are evident in both their behavior and their capacity for situational adaptation. The 11th factor is ownership of policy execution, particularly among policy leaders. Due to the complementing talents and competence of the project team members, the implementation is significantly influenced. The 12th factor is this. This is done to mobilize the army around a shared objective.

Thirteenth, the execution may be impacted by the distinction between the function of political leaders or ministers and that of civil officials. Roles that overlap might have detrimental consequences. The 14th factor is the capacity of the personnel participating in the implementation stage. Their skill is dependent on the depth of experience, education, and credentials held by the participants. Active stakeholder discussions, especially those with the affected parties and organizations, are crucial to the implementation of policies. This is the 15th factor.

The sixteenth component is trust, which provides an atmosphere that is supportive of implementation. The utilization of networks that make use of one's access and maintain control over resources constitutes the 17th element. More comprehensive help for implementation is offered by this. The people's values and beliefs serve as the last 18th component. This embodies the belief that new policy measures are "good" and "correct," respectively. A new policy is also disowned if it goes against the group's core values or beliefs.

Factors in Nepal

Poor design during formulation, poor coordination between complementary programs, and careless resource allocation have all proven damaging in Nepal. Politicians and public workers play overlapping responsibilities, with ministers showing interest in micromanagement and bureaucrats in policy management. The involvement of the development partner is another aspect. They thrive as long as contributors continue to be generous with their cherished policies. Similar to how attitude issues like rent-seeking and corruption have destroyed some rules. The lack of leadership commitment to policy has pierced a number of implementation strategies.

In many instances, policies have been left orphaned by frequent changes in key offices like secretaries or ministers. Super-versus-non- super ministries syndrome is a problem for government ministries. This has made it difficult to coordinate across ministries. Additionally, it appears that overconfidence has increased, rocking many policy boats. Setting a realistic goal is generally good because of this. The "no- problem" management approach is sometimes ingrained in implementers. The corporate culture is notorious for its poor delivery performance.

Failures of policies have been attributed to a mismatch between available and needed human resources. The general level of public trust in political leadership is still low. Because people have little faith in the government, privatization has suffered. Even though many public businesses cannot function in their existing form, no one dares to privatize them since privatization has lost its legitimacy. The last distinctive element in Nepal is "geopolitics." Simply because of the idea that "geopolitics" is waiting like an enraged elephant on the road ahead, it hinders the nation's great initiatives.

Need for research

The society in Nepal is also aware that some policies are useless or full of folly, but they persist unabated. Some participants in politics hunger after failed initiatives. The others are forced to put up with their whims. Some of these obnoxious regulations catch on and affect the federal, provincial, and municipal levels of government. Among them are the user's committee in development schemes, farm subsidies, and election area development programs. They resemble gaps in the country's financial system through which public funds are distributed to cronies and political operatives.

The list of elements above is only the tip of the iceberg. It would be dangerous to confirm the degree to which any variable is active in Nepal's policy corridors without empirical testing. There is an alarming dearth of studies on the application of policy throughout the nation. May domestic organizations like the National Planning Commission, Policy Research Institute, and universities bravely get to work right now.

Chapter 10: Success Stories of Business in Nepal

The majority of Nepalese youngsters are emigrating overseas to seek better career possibilities and a more promising future for themselves. The majority of them blame the fact that instability and insecurity are prevalent across Nepal and that there is no certainty of a good future. If we look at the present scenario in Nepal from the outside, these perspectives seem to be correct. Nonetheless, many underground businesses prosper in our nation, Nepal, despite the difficulties and instability they face. Because of this, they have shown that there are always hidden chances in any unpleasant situation, provided that we have a strong desire to achieve something with a clear goal and resolve.

10.1 Thrilling Tales of Three Nepali Female Entrepreneurs

While none of them intended to become social entrepreneurs, a series of events and realizations in the lives of three Nepali female entrepreneurs pushed them in that direction. One woman found inspiration in her grandmother's knitting abilities, which had not received the recognition they deserved. The desire was to use her public health education to make a difference in the lives of individuals in rural parts of Nepal who were unaware of the importance of nutrition and menstrual hygiene. In the third case, the female entrepreneur had always wanted to do something for her nation, so she drew inspiration from her undergraduate internship in a hamlet and began her entrepreneurial adventure with homemade items. "My connection to my grandparents, as well as the things I have learned from them, the tales they have told me, their wisdom, and everything else, has motivated me to become who I am today."[93] Since she was a toddler, Lorina Sthapit, co-founder of Aji's had cherished wearing garments made by her grandmother's expert and experienced hands. Her grandmother used to knit socks and gloves and give them out to family and friends, and she grew up in that tradition. As Lorina got older, she recognized how vital her grandmother's abilities were and decided to assist her in receiving the respect she deserved. She came across other outstanding old artists whose abilities she believed should be passed on to the next generation of artisans in her labor[94].

The aged have essential talents, but they also have remarkable and exceptional life tales and experiences to share with the younger generation. While she was a youngster, she recalls her grandfather's narrative of his long voyage to Lhasa for commerce, which piqued her interest. Those tales have significant cultural and historical significance, but they have not been recorded or passed on to future generations. Lorina was certain that all of these tales and abilities would be lost to history if she didn't do anything. As envisioned by the founder, Aji's Products and the Aji's Podcast were born out of the desire to encourage older people to live healthier and happier lives[95]. Working at Aji's, Lorina is obtaining business skills, but she is also developing the intuition, bravery, and compassion necessary when dealing with the elderly. Aji's ideals are very similar to those of her grandparents because of their strong relationship.

93 https://www.scmp.com/video/asia/3111968/nepal-traditional-crafts-made-elderly-arti- sans-get-online-spotlight
94 https://www.thejakartapost.com/life/2020/11/30/handmade-with-love-nepali-takes-grand- mas-socks-to-the-world.html
95 https://podcasts.apple.com/us/podcast/ajis-podcast/id1480995250

"Given the significance, my mother placed on education and goals, I have developed into a person who pursues the things she desires."

Bonita Sharma learned the hard way that sometimes the best way to navigate life is to stumble along and eventually find your way[96]. This is exactly what happened to her. Bonita visited a town in Terai a few weeks ago, where she met a lady who created and sold homemade wine to make a livelihood. The lady, who lived in a tiny hut, didn't have enough food to feed herself and her companion at home. Despite this, she was anxious to give Bonita a taste of her dish, which she gladly accepted. Her ultimate objective in life, no matter how impoverished she was in terms of fundamental requirements such as education, food, and health, was to gather enough resources to educate her two kids and prepare them to be self-sufficient in their adult lives. This tenacity and the acts of generosity and altruism performed at the grassroots level motivate Bonita every day and makes her realize that there is still much more that can be done to assist these self-motivated women in the neighborhood. Bonita's adventure began with a nutrition education campaign in the neighborhood, which she carried out with the help of other youngsters and creative tools such as the Nutrias bracelet. Following a flurry of positive replies and expressions of gratitude for their efforts, Bonita decided to launch a full-fledged social enterprise to assist, educate, and reach out to even more women. However, it's far easier said than done in practice. She launched Social Changemakers and Innovators (Sochai) as a non-profit organization[97]. Still, as her journey progressed, she became more aware of the need for social entrepreneurship and understood that there is no such thing as a free meal. The experience of running a social company has further extended her horizons and assisted her in making connections with inspiring women on a local level, which helps keep her grounded and motivated. A former public health student who became a social

---

96 https://www.unesco.org/en/articles/bonita-young-change-maker-inspires-girls-and-women- nepal-through-education
97 https://sochai.org/about/

entrepreneur has taken a holistic approach to empower these women by providing them with education on menstrual hygiene and nutrition and skills such as making handicraft bracelets and affordable, nutritious food to help them become more self-sufficient[98].

"When I arrived at that isolated farm in Nepal, I discovered that the farmer was running his farm entirely on his initiative. And it occurred to me that if someone from so far away as Kathmandu can do this, why shouldn't we be able to? It opened my eyes to the fact that there is a plethora of issues that may be tackled with an entrepreneurial approach." After enrolling in a Master of Business Administration degree at King's College, Rosana Shrestha developed an entrepreneurial attitude. During her undergraduate years, she learned about major corporations like Apple and Google. Still, during her two-month internship at Gummi, she came to comprehend and appreciate the genuine spirit and meaning of entrepreneurship for the first time. Rosana's eyes were opened when she saw a farmer manage to accomplish everything independently, despite the many obstacles and lack of basic amenities and infrastructure. It was a life-changing experience. She returned with new enthusiasm, a different skill set, and a whole lot of coffee, all of which would transform her life for the better. Her passion for crafting DIY items and home cures led her to create body scrubs from the coffee she had obtained from Gummi, which she enjoyed using. This provided her with the opportunity to create a business that she is passionate about. The Nuga company now has more than nine product lines that are 100 percent organic and natural and devoid of preservatives. More importantly, even if it is a tiny step, she has realized a childhood desire to contribute to the economy and dispel the stereotype of Nepal as an impoverished nation by starting this business.

10.2 Young Entrepreneurs of Nepal

In recent years, young Nepali entrepreneurs have been setting the road to creating employment and possibilities. What does it take

---

98 https://kathmandupost.com/author/bonita-sharma

to establish a company in Nepal, and how long does it take? Is it merely about having a lot of money, talented people, or handling legal procedures? I have interviewed and spoken with entrepreneurs about their perspectives on this issue and found that when it comes to e-commerce, the most significant obstacles in Nepal are unregistered businesses that conduct haphazard operations and leave a negative image on the market. Unhealthy business practices in our e-commerce sector include product variants, inadequate delivery services, and exorbitant prices for items, to name a few. The additional issues include a lack of cash, a shortage of educated labor, the high cost of advertising, and a high turnover rate in the field of human resources. The process of forming a corporation is not complex. However, there are situations when superfluous or excessive documentation is required, and the legal procedure may be highly time- consuming and complicated. Certain activities take place "below the table." Establishing an innovative enterprise in a third-world nation such as ours is difficult since most of your family and relatives will be opposed to what you are trying to do. They urge you to either relocate overseas or take a well-paying government position in your own country. Without sufficient cash to start or expand your company, obtaining financing to start or expand your firm would be challenging. Gathering information on your market, clients, and comparable products/services that already exist is a challenging task as it is difficult to uncover previous records. The announcement of an occasional strike might have ramifications for a company's supply chain and other activities. Legal processes are not difficult to understand. The majority of the business registration process may be completed online. So far, our consumers are pleased with the goods and services provided, but they would want to see the number of locations increase.

Despite having dedicated and passionate personnel, one of the most significant hurdles in establishing a worldwide firm in this country is a lack of labor and infrastructure. The companies have folks who have degrees but lack the necessary basic experiences. For enterprises in Nepal, having a reliable internet connection has been a problem. Our legal procedure is not difficult to understand. Eventually, you'll have to settle with a conservative approach to taxation and corporate practices. Depending on the kind of investment, there are sound rules in place. It is often the bureaucrats and their unwillingness to cooperate that contribute to the complexity of the legal procedure. Though it is relatively simple to locate prospects to start a project in Nepal, the route to achieving a solid solution is not without its difficulties. Every firm needs the assistance or product of other companies at some point in its journey. For a thriving economy, every node of these networks must be in good working order for new enterprises to develop.

As a prospective entrepreneur in Nepal, you will quickly discover that the vast majority of the nodes in this network are non-existent. Companies that are just getting started are confronted with an automatic feeling of dependence on other nations, which, in turn, undervalues innovation at the local level and the mobilization of local assets. There are several challenges that one must deal with while working in government agencies. On top of that, when it comes to legal criteria, the scarcity of relevant and up-to-date information on the process for incorporation, sources of finance, regulatory frameworks, and other similar issues is a substantial roadblock. They are also out of the current in reflecting the many sorts of technology firms growing in the Nepali market, resulting in uncertainty and confusion for consumers.

Given that some product is attempting to actualize a system in which local resources and local talent may grow and flourish in a sustainable environment, it has aided them in developing a good brand identity. However, they are grateful that the customer sector, in contrast to the majority of enterprises in Nepal, is not concentrated in the valley, allowing them to communicate and implement their suggestions. The most difficult obstacles to overcome when establishing a project in Nepal are the lack of a product and a consumer. Understanding whether or not your product has a market and whether or not you can effectively manufacture the product is similarly tough to determine. Finding the proper individuals to work with is often a hurdle when starting a business. If you have a product and a market, the problem is figuring out how to get your product in front of them. At Unelma Platforms, they have primary business plan has been to acquire clients via excellent service, with word-of-mouth accounting for around 60 percent of their total customer base. They helped to get the word out about their goods. People like personalizing their creations, and the process of conceptualizing a design and having it made is a thrilling experience. Capital is crucial, but I believe it should be considered a secondary criterion. The legal procedure is extensive, and it takes time for the system to be set up. It is never simple to start a business, and one of the most difficult challenges is gaining the confidence of employees and other stakeholders. It occurred to me often when I was a teenager. When people enquire about my age, it appears to be more difficult to trust what I am telling them. There are many obstacles to overcome, and there are few mentors to help us. If you are doing business without registering, you will not encounter any difficulties; nevertheless, once you register, difficulties will arise.

There are currently no regulations or processes in place to govern social entrepreneurship in Nepal. Legal processes for non-profit organizations are not difficult to navigate in the first place, but tax procedures are time-consuming. They haven't done any market research since they are not a manufacturing company but rather a service-oriented organization with products ranging from flight booking, online reservation, custom and tailored made software and AI-based products. They have a small number of clients in the accelerating and consulting fields that they serve. So far, they've received a lot of excellent feedback.

It seems that first and foremost, you must persuade yourself that you can successfully establish and operate a business in Nepal. A core team for a firm is tough to develop since, after a given amount of time, individuals desire to travel and work in other countries. People in this area lack patience and are only interested in short-term rewards. These intangible qualities, like learning and personal growth, are not valued by them. Nepal comes in at number 94th on the World Bank's ranking of the ease of doing business. If you are just starting, it might be quite difficult to navigate the system. Most young entrepreneurs continue to feel that our legal procedure may be enhanced and streamlined so that any aspiring or current entrepreneurs do not have to go through unnecessary headaches merely to establish and manage a firm in the first place. For example, because some of them are a branding firm, most of the customers with whom they work are unfamiliar with the term "branding."

Educating about the product is also vital in Nepalese market because of overall literary rate. Some business owners feel that they must hold a workshop merely to educate customers about their products, and this happens from time to time. It is well worth it since customer feel the service, they give benefits their clients and businesses. Although organic goods are becoming more popular in today's society, it is very difficult to produce them without synthetic ingredients. In all honesty, meeting global market requirements is challenging. Still, they view this as a chance to enhance efforts by using local resources, with their taste and contour adding to an original flavor to the goods and services they provide. Their initiative to give tourists warm hospitality while also providing them with a view of the coffee farm seems to have been a success. Many young entrepreneurs received positive feedback from a diverse range of visitors. In terms of setup, the local community has been helpful, and they have also assisted entrepreneurs in the marketing of the coffee farm, for example. However, the restricted market and the risks connected with new ideas have proven to be significant roadblocks for many of them.

Chapter 11: The Best Finance Companies in Nepal

The development of Nepal's financial firms is critical to the country's economic growth in the long run. Recently, there has been a significant amount of reformation in the Nepali banking industry. The number of A-class commercial banks is expanding, but so is the number of C-class financial institutions being established. In Nepal, there are tens of thousands of such establishments. While most of us think of financial institutions as merely a corporation dealing with the deposit and withdrawal of money, the word refers to a far larger range of activities. Finance businesses are tiny financial institutions founded to meet the short-term financial needs of their clients and consumers. Nepal has many financial institutions, which is a good thing. Nepal's finance businesses are classified as C-grade financial institutions, which means the Nepal Rastra Bank licenses them. They are formed to meet the demands of clients at a more localized and less expensive level. The financial firm has played a vital role in Nepal's income creation, entrepreneurial growth, and women's empowerment, among other areas. Several finance businesses in Nepal have now established themselves in rural regions and assist the local population.

Corporations have a significant influence in raising the living standards of individuals living in rural regions. Some financial institutions also provide online banking services, which enable customers to access their accounts via e-Sewa[99]. Users may reload their NTC and Ncell accounts online. Some companies now offer consumers the option of using a debit card. The following is a list of some financial institutions in Nepal. The term refers to a specialized monetary organization that provides credit for purchasing consumer goods and offers by purchasing time-scales contracts from merchants or by giving modest loans to customers directly.

When your money is on the line, you want to make the most informed decision possible. There are a variety of aspects that contribute to the success of a financial organization. So, without further ado, here are the five top financing businesses in Nepal, listed in no particular order. In this chapter, I have compiled a list of the greatest financial firms in Nepal that are now functioning in the city from among the hundreds of such establishments.

11.1 Shree Investment Finance Co. Ltd

The headquarters of Shree Investment & Financial Co Ltd are located in Kathmandu's Dilli Bazar district. Shree was founded in 1994 by a group of prominent businesspeople from Kathmandu. Since then, they have been drawing customers in with exceptional offers and providing a dependable service. For additional information about their programmers and services, please visit their website. The Shree Investment and Financial Institution is a "C" Class Financial Institution that is licensed by Nepal Rastra Bank. This organization has achieved success in the financial sector of Nepal via hard work and perseverance, and it has seen significant development over the last several years. Because of this, the firm is always developing and evolving new goods and services to meet customer needs.

To be consistently innovative and adaptable to changes to meet consumer requests and deliver excellent services to investors,

---

99 https://esewa.com.np/

shareholders, stakeholders, and customers. The firm now has seven department offices outside of the Kathmandu Valley. According to the company's website, the headquarter is situated in Kathmandu, to expand to other parts of the nation soon.

11.2 Lalitpur Finance Ltd

Lalitpur Finance, often known as LAFIN, is another well-known financial organization in Nepal that you can rely on. Its headquarters are located at Lagan Khel, in the state of Lalitpur. They have managed to maintain their prominence by continual innovation and dynamic tactics tailored to the specific needs of consumers and clients. Since its inception, it has been able to get positive feedback from customers. Established following the Financing Firm Act of 2043, Lalitpur Finance Ltd. Lalitpur Finance is the first private sector finance company that the Lalitpur District wholly owns. It has been possible for this firm to accomplish its functions and is now doing so extremely well under the leadership of Nepal Rastra Bank.

The financial performance of this company demonstrates its enduring strength as a consequence of its abilities. On September 18, 2020, Lalitpur Finance was also listed on the Nepal Stock Exchange, which was the first time the company had done so. Transparency, accountability, statistical disclosures, and strict ethical practices are all hallmarks of Lalitpur Finance Ltd. (Lafon), and they have now become the company's distinguishing characteristics. However, throughout the years, Lalitpur Finance has also assisted us in gaining the trust of investors by implementing the notions outlined above. LAFIN assists consumers from a variety of companies and homes by providing them with new monetary goods and solutions and assisting them in realizing their ambitions. Lalitpur Finance is a diverse economic services firm whose success is based on responding quickly, creatively, and effectively to its clients' needs.

11.3 Other Banks in Nepal

United Finance Limited is yet another well-known brand in Nepal, and a well-known businessperson in the country markets it. Its headquarters are in Kathmandu's Durbar Marg district. Its mission is to offer a comprehensive solution to all of the banking demands of its clients via continual development. Founded in 2051 BS (Bikram Sambat) as a national-level financial organization, it has been in existence since then. Jebels finance has also been established with the help of a group of experts from a variety of backgrounds. From the beginning, it has provided services to a diverse range of consumers. The company's headquarters are situated on New Road, and branch offices may be found all around the nation. Established in 2049 BS to assist society, Nepal Finance Limited (also known as NEFINSCO) is the country's first private sector- run finance company. They claim to be a trailblazer in the fields of hire purchase and margin lending, among other things. The prudential finance corporation was created on Baisakh 16th, 2061, and has been in operation since then. Its headquarters are in Shanti Marg, Kathmandu, Nepal, and it has branches all around the country, including the United States. It is considered to be one of the greatest financial institutions in Nepal.

They aspire to assist people from all walks of life and be the finest in the business when it comes to delivering financial services to the general public. It was created in 2051 B.S. as Kathmandu Finance Limited (KFL), also known as Gurkhas Finance. The organization's ultimate goal is to continuously enhance the quality of its products and services while providing superior service to its customers. With a variety of plans and incentives for clients, the banking industry has acquired the confidence of its most valuable customers. It is considered to be one of the greatest financial institutions in Nepal. Since its inception, it has strived to offer its consumers a comprehensive range of financial products. The company's headquarters are situated in Dillibazzar on Charkhal Road. ICFC Finance was established in 2018 following the provisions of the Company Act 2053.

Its headquarters are in Kathmandu, Nepal, and it has branches throughout the nation, including the country's capital city. The financial firm is also managed by a group of highly skilled experts from a variety of backgrounds. They are primarily concerned with the financial requirements of small and medium-sized businesses. The International Capital Financing Corporation (ICFC) is one of the top finance businesses in Nepal. After being established under the Financial Company Act 2042, Nepal Rastra Bank (NRB) granted the company a license to do business as a financial organization on January 1, 2051. When it comes to financial services, this organization is the leader, thanks to a unique blend of passion and concept implementation. With the creativity and foresight of providing excellent financial services for achievement. According to the company's website, the authorized capital is Rupees 1,000,000,000/- and the issued capital is Rupees 800,000,000/-. According to the SEC, the promoter owns 51 percent of the Paid-Up Capital, with the remaining 49 percent being owned by the general public. Its stock is traded on the Nepal Stock Exchange Limited (NEPSE). Sunrise Bank Limited is "Rising to Serve" in an economy driven by a desire for success, and this is being accomplished through establishing new levels of product and service offerings. As a bank created by well-known businesspeople, they understand the needs of an expanding economy and are well-equipped to meet those needs. Stockholders, depositors, consumers, and other stakeholders have high expectations of the company.

The bank has committed to working tirelessly to achieve its goals by continuing to be a leader in banking on all fronts and by expanding its footprint both inside and beyond the nation, among other things. By focusing on under-served or feasible provider sectors like as SMEs and retail enterprises, among others. Using environmentally friendly and knowledgeable personnel, they have remodeled and reconstructed the bank's infrastructures and systems, which they have maintained. The Civil bank was established with the goal and vision of establishing itself as the most trusted financial institution by providing committed services to all of its customers. It was started by a group of promoters who came from various professional backgrounds and so were able to provide services to people from all walks of life and all sections of society through enabling financial progress. The Civil Bank asserts that it is not a game and here to stay; they have zero tolerance for violations of rules, policies, norms, and prudential banking standards, and they have a strong conviction in their ability to maintain their moral business ideals. Together with its promoter and shareholders, the bank is committed to creating value for all stakeholders via cutting-edge technology and banking science.

11.4 Perfect Time to Invest in Nepal

For far too long, the business potential of Nepal has been underappreciated and overlooked. Investment in Nepal was always a hazardous business since the country had been engulfed in political upheaval for over two decades. However, since the political goal has now correctly switched towards economic development, and due to the establishment of a stable administration, Nepal has emerged as the ideal location for foreign investment. After achieving GDP growth of 7.5 percent once, the signals of a resurgent economy have already begun to manifest themselves. In recent years, there have been considerable changes from the government in removing severe power outages and drafting legislation favorable to investment. The dramatic growth in Foreign Direct Investment in Nepal is a strong indication that it is past time to take advantage of the economic boom that is now taking place in Nepal. Hydropower, tourism, and the cement industry are all prospering right now.

The service sector and small and medium-sized firms (SMEs) aren't far behind in reaping the benefits of the country's fast increase in commercial activity, which has occurred concurrently with infrastructure construction. The entrepreneurial movement in Nepal is gaining momentum, and young entrepreneurs with huge aspirations are emerging in the country, whose contributions may be felt immediately across all sectors. Because of the vast potential and low labor cost, investing in an unsaturated market would almost certainly provide a larger return on investment than participating in any saturated market. Two decades of political upheaval culminated in the formation of the Central Government, which was devoted to promoting foreign direct investment and economic activity. Economic concerns are a big component of the agendas of all political parties nowadays. People's livelihoods are being improved by a stable province and an enthusiastic local administration focused and devoted to this goal. Earlier this month, the government of Nepal signed a Memorandum of Understanding (MOU) on the framework agreement for China's One Belt One Road Initiative (OBOR)[100]. The government of Nepal is committed to improving connectivity with both neighboring countries via road and railway construction. Having joined the South Asian Free Trade Area (SAFTA) and the Bay of Bengal Initiative for Multi-Sectoral Technical and Economic Cooperation (BIMSTEC) Free Trade Agreement[101], it enjoys the benefits of tariff and tax exemption. In the World Bank's 'Ease of Doing Business Report 2021,' Nepal was placed third among South Asian nations, behind only Bhutan and India. Nepal has recently amended its laws and regulations to make them more investment-friendly, and it is now engaged in the process of continual development. In most areas, foreign investors are permitted to hold 100 percent of the company.

A more favorable business environment is created through the Bilateral Investment Promotion and Protection Agreement (BIPPA), which has been signed with Finland, India, Germany, Mauritius, Qatar,

---

100 Chinese Investments in Nepal in the Context of BRI.
   https://www.vifindia.org/article/2019/ october/11/chinese-investments-in-nepal-in-the-context-of-bri
101 Bay of Bengal Initiative for Multi-Sectoral Technical and Economic,
   https://commerce.gov.in/ international-trade/trade-agreements/indias-current-engagements-in-rtas/bay-of-bengal-ini- tiative-for-multi-sectoral-technical-and-economic-cooperation-bimstec-free-trade-agree- ment-fta-negotiations-as-of-july-2014/

the United Kingdom, and France. Australia, China, India, Korea, Mauritius, Norway, Pakistan, Qatar, Sri Lanka and Thailand have all signed a Double Taxation Avoidance Agreement. Nepal is sandwiched between two of the world's greatest economies, both of which have seen a rapid economic expansion in recent years: India and China. It has access to a market with a total population of nearly 2.7 billion people. Open borders and duty-free commerce with India and duty-free access to China for over eight thousand items are among the benefits of this arrangement. The government has taken the initiative to increase the technical ability and competency of the workforce, which is essential for fast economic growth. The working population accounts for 61 percent of the total population of twenty-eight million people. The participation of women in the South Asian population is fairly high when compared to other nations. The labor costs are reasonable.

Where Should You Put Your Money? Being the world's second-richest nation in terms of hydroelectricity potential, Nepal has a promising future in this industry. Nepal has a huge number of steep, everlasting rivers supported by its topographical inclination; the building of enormous hydroelectricity projects is a possibility in the country. Because Nepal is a developing country with limited financial resources, resources have not been used to their full potential. In addition, India, Nepal's southern neighbor, will always need clean and affordable energy, ensuring that there will always be a market for Nepal's hydroelectric power projects. With more than six thousand big and small perennial rivers running across Nepal, including the three main rivers, the Koshi, the Gandaki, and the Karnali, there is tremendous potential for hydropower development in the country. Nepal is a landlocked nation with a diverse geographical landscape, making transportation a significant challenge. As a result, there is an urgent need for adequate transportation infrastructure. There is also a need for various modes of transportation, including cable transportation, railroads, and water transportation, among others. In part due to the country's geographical diversity, there is a scarcity of roads throughout the country, and even the roads in urban areas are in poor condition and in need of expansion; as a result, improving existing roads and funding new road projects are top priorities for the government, making this an excellent venture to invest in.

The presence of a massive mountain range is advantageous to cable transportation operations. In addition, railways have a significant potential for displacing other modes of transportation in the southern plain region. Just one international airport is a serious concern, but it also presents significant commercial potential. Transportation projects with large budgets are the ideal area in which to invest in Nepal. The agriculture sector, which accounts for the majority of the country's gross domestic product (GDP), is the dominant force in the economy. Until 2017, agriculture was the primary source of income for the majority of the population. Today, agriculture provides a secondary source of income for a smaller proportion of the population. A huge part of the populace believes that agriculture as a company is not a lucrative activity. Nepal is well-suited for agriculture due to its geographic and physical location, as well as its favorable climatic circumstances. This is also a positive element when it comes to cultivating and harvesting uncommon medicinal plants. New technologies that contribute to agriculture are very uncommon, making the possibility of implementing these technologies in Nepal a significant investment opportunity.

Production of cash crops as a business concept can be a successful venture in Nepal, where commercial agricultural initiatives are still in their early stages. Having a diversified geographical environment and a highly rich and diverse cultural heritage, Nepal receives a large number of visitors, making tourism the country's most important industry. Eight of the world's ten tallest peaks and other mountain ranges can be found in the country, making it a popular destination for mountaineers, rock climbers, hikers, and those looking for outdoor adventure opportunities.

Nepal is the birthplace of Buddha and the site of several Hindu and Buddhist temples, resulting in many pilgrims visiting the country on an annual basis. Every year, many archaeologists come to study the temples and structures that date back thousands of years and are of great archaeological significance. Tourism in Nepal is growing exponentially, with international visitors spending an average of 11.78 days in the country. Another factor contributing to the potential rise of tourism is the region's distinctive flora and wildlife.

Every year, in one of Nepal's most isolated regions, a new attraction, a new wildness, and a new experience unfolds before our eyes. In addition, the nation has a large number of competent porters and guides that might be employed for a very modest price. These elements combine to make tourism one of the most promising sectors in which to invest in Nepal. The country is in desperate need of infrastructure development, which is one of its most pressing demands. The huge earthquake that struck Nepal in 2015 caused widespread devastation in the Kathmandu valley and surrounding regions, highlighting the urgent need to develop earthquake- resistant infrastructures in these and other places. Because transportation infrastructure needs significant repair, this might be an area to consider investing in as well.

The Nepalese government has always been supportive of investors attempting to establish themselves in the infrastructure industry. The information technology sector has taken over the globe at this moment, and Nepal is no exception. Nepal has a large number of highly qualified IT graduates who may be employed at very low salaries. New skills and ideas will likely be explored because it is a fresh area of interest in the Nepalese context. IT firms are developing as a new business endeavor; thus, the competition will be less intense if you decide to invest now. Nepal is located in the heart of the Himalayan Belt, which means it has a tremendous amount of mineral wealth. The Himalayan area is comprised of mineral clusters that include both metallic and nonmetallic minerals.

Nepal is also well-known for exporting a variety of stunning ornamental stones, many of which are imported. Despite the availability of large quantities of minerals distributed over the Himalayan range, Nepal has not harvested these minerals due to a lack of infrastructure. The number of current mineral extraction enterprises is limited, and they are not very effective. Investors have several prospects to make investments in cement factories, lime extraction, coal, magnetize, talc clay, and other related industries. As a result, if someone chooses to invest in this area, it could be a highly successful business venture in Nepal.

Nepal's healthcare system is in a very precarious position. It will need a great deal of improvisation and development. Similarly, the education sector is much behind the times. Every year, many students go overseas to pursue higher education. These should be compelling arguments for investing in Nepal. With the increase in population and the expansion of industry and technology, telecommunications have become an increasingly important need.

There are just a few telecommunications firms in Nepal, which means there is less competition in the market. Because of the difficult geographical circumstances in the nation, even the current networks have not been able to reach the most isolated locations. There is an enormous potential for anybody looking to start a lucrative company in Nepal due to this development. Nepal is working toward a more flexible foreign investment policy and attempting to establish an investment-friendly climate to attract more foreign investment. The Nepalese government strongly encourages foreign investment, whether in the form of joint venture operations with Nepalese investors or the form of 100 percent foreign-owned firms. In addition to having one of the most favorable tax environments and ease of doing business globally, Nepal is one of the most attractive investment locations for Nepalese and foreign investors.

Chapter 12: Ecommerce in Nepal

It has been more than two decades since e-commerce first gained traction in the country. By now, there are hundreds of e-commerce websites operating in Nepal, thanks to the progress of information technology and its widespread use. As of August, last year, Nepal had more than 40,000 business websites registered with the government. During the last several years, many Nepalese have acclimated to the convenience of internet shopping. Furthermore, during the recent lockdown implemented to restrict the spread of the Covid-19 virus, the popularity and relevance of e-commerce websites has increased, and it's only going to grow further. As a result, the rivalry among e-commerce websites has become fiercer than ever. Amid this environment, certain e-commerce websites have been successful in establishing their presence in the market.

Regularly, you may have seen adverts for various products and services while reading through your Facebook, Instagram, or even Tiktok timeline. These commercials enable you to place an order and complete the transaction. Commercial transactions have been feasible with the growth of information technology, which has accompanied the rise of the Internet. As a result, several businesses in Nepal, like Daraz[102],

---

102 https://www.daraz.com.np/

Sastodeal[103], and UG Bazaar[104], have benefited from the availability of e-commerce opportunities. These days, the digital form of conducting commercial transactions via the internet, also known as e-commerce, has attracted the attention of Nepal's urban young.

With the outbreak of the Covid-19 virus[105], the relevance of e-commerce has been brought to the attention of both the public and business owners. Consequently, one may be curious about when and how this business model, which has been showing its usefulness to the maximum extent possible in this unprecedented time, came into being and reached this stage today. The creation of CompuServe in 1969 marked the beginning of the history of electronic commerce across the globe. In 1984, the same firm, which is widely regarded as the world's first significant e-commerce organization, established Electronic Mall, which enabled its customers to purchase from more than a hundred online stores and merchants. It was the world's first instance of internet selling, and it was a huge success. E-commerce is thriving all over the globe, and it is now experiencing a boom. With the introduction of e-commerce in Nepal, Nepalis living abroad will send presents to their family and friends and relatives who live in the country. The transition from traditional brick- and-mortar retailers to online stores started in late 2000. Bal Krishna Joshi, one of the co-founders of Thamel.com, says that his firm is the country's first-ever e-commerce venture.

12.1 Ecommerce Sites of Nepal

Daraz is, without a doubt, the most popular e-commerce website in Nepal. This website, which was first launched in Nepal in 2014 and then bought by Alibaba Group in 2018, has already garnered more than 100,000 users[106]. Daraz is an online marketplace that links thousands of

103 https://www.sastodeal.com/
104 https://www.ugbazaar.com/
105 Full article: Face mask recognition system using MobileNetV2
     https://www.tandfonline.com/ doi/full/10.1080/08839514.2022.2145638
106 https://kathmandupost.com/miscellaneous/2018/05/09/alibaba-makes-forays-into-nepal

vendors with prospective customers who want to buy their products. Daraz offers access to about 500,000 goods in more than a hundred categories, including food, fashion, electronics, home appliances, and other items, and it sends more than 200,000 deliveries every month to customers. It is also worth mentioning that Custodial is another e-commerce site that has successfully attracted thousands of clients, suppliers and partners in Nepal.

Recent collaborations with Myntra and Flipkart, two well-known e-commerce sites in India, have also been announced. Sastodeal provides its consumers with a wide range of items, including food, clothes, home appliances, and electronics, sourced from thousands of small businesses and independent sellers. The company also guarantees the return and exchange of the merchandise within a certain time frame.

Approximately 800,000 unique users each month come to Daraz's website, according to its site statistics[107]. It is a free virtual platform that allows its users, whether they are individuals or businesses, to enlist a broad variety of new and secondhand items to purchase and sell them on the internet. This website facilitates the exchange of information between merchants and prospective consumers. It allows its customers to purchase and sell a wide variety of new and used things, ranging from fashion and accessories to vacation and tour packages, according to their preferences. When Daraz was launched in 2014 as an online directory of items and stores in the Kathmandu valley, it was considered a success. Today, it is a popular online marketplace for people in Nepal. Daraz has hundreds of stores around the nation, and its products are available online. Nepal describes itself as an e-commerce powerhouse because it currently serves more than five thousand businesses through an ecosystem of solutions and services provided by five different companies under their parent organization, the 'Thule Group.'

Foodmandu is a popular e-commerce site among foodies in the

---

107 https://nepaldatabase.com/evolution-of-e-commerce-and-daraz-in-nepal

Kathmandu valley[108]. Foodmandu allows its customers to purchase meals and dishes from hundreds of restaurants around the valley, and the foods and dishes they order will be brought right to their doorsteps. Currently, there are no other meal delivery applications that can compete with Foodmandu's level of popularity. Foodmandu likewise made a point of demonstrating its existence during the shutdown by altering its business strategy and forming a partnership with merchants. In addition, it started delivering fresh food, such as fruits and vegetables, to clients' houses. This has further enhanced the company's already well-established reputation in Nepal's e-commerce environment.

12.2 What is the current scenario of the e-commerce business in Nepal?

Online shopping in Nepal goes back to 2002, when muncha.com were launched in the same year. During Dashain, the website was used to sell Khasi (goats) online. Nepalis residing abroad would order Khasi for their relatives back home and pay for it (remit the money). The website will then transport the Khasi to the doorstep of the customer's family after collecting the payment. Even though it was restricted to the Kathmandu Valley, this marked the beginning of the e-commerce sector in Nepal. Currently, Nepal has just a handful of e-commerce websites that are actively running (Kathmandu, to be more specific). They are mostly concerned with the Kathmandu valley. A large number of internet stores are now beginning to operate outside of Kathmandu also. Some lesser- known examples include: social networking site such as e-Sathi.com. Daraz operates distribution networks in Butwal, Biratnagar, Pokhara, and several other significant towns and cities in Nepal.

Furthermore, several firms, such as Daraz and others, have their unique ecommerce system in existence. These are essentially extensions to their current locations and delivery mechanisms, rather than a full-fledged

---

108 https://foodmandu.com/

online store in the traditional sense. We don't have precise information on those online marketplaces' total investment, transaction, and profit. Still, we can safely infer that they are experiencing difficulties in several areas, the most significant of which are delivery and refund policies. Daraz, the largest of Nepal's online retailers, claims to have had 800,000 visits in a single month and expects to get an average of 2500,000 visits per month in the next three to four years. If the claims are correct, this is a respectable quantity of traffic. What matters is how many of these visitors' become customers. There are several types of e-Commerce business models[109].

Allow me to describe the most often used ones: The B2B model stands for Business to Business. This is when the platform functions as a go-between for different types of enterprises. Typically, such platforms enable retail enterprises to purchase in bulk from manufacturers. Alibaba, India Mart, and other large B2B platforms are examples of this. The B2C Model (Business to Customer) is the most frequent sort of business plan for an e-commerce site. Businesses in this sector offer their goods directly to the final customer. B2C e-commerce platforms include sites such as AliExpress, Daraz, and Sastodeal, among others. A consumer- to-consumer ecommerce (customer to customer) business model in which the platform serves as a conduit between consumers. eBay, and other such sites are examples. Alternatively known as consumer-to- business ecommerce, the C2B model is a kind of online retailing in which businesses sell to other businesses. With this shift, the old paradigm is completely turned on its head, with individuals who would ordinarily be end consumers, generating products and services consumed by the companies and organizations from whom they purchase their goods and services. The term "hybrid ecommerce" refers to a platform that integrates two or more previously described modes of commerce. Amazon is a good illustration of this.

109 5 E-commerce Business Models - NerdWallet.
https://www.nerdwallet.com/article/small-busi- ness/e-commerce-models

12.3 What are the challenges of ecommerce?

Many Nepalese people have a lot of spare time on their hands. They can stroll to the shop and purchase items at any moment. This is one of the most difficulties facing the ecommerce industry. The majority of the time, shopping is done in groups. Whenever someone has to purchase anything, they will go to the store with a group of pals. An additional problem for ecommerce sites is the user's perception of their purchase. Another significant difficulty is delivery. Technology and technological iliteracy can be a problem. People are just utilizing ecommerce sites to check costs so that they may haggle when purchasing a product from a physical dealer in person. As a result, they are more often utilized as a reference tool than as a purchasing platform. There is a scarcity of credit cards and wallet systems.

Nevertheless, the availability of several e-wallet providers such as E-Sewa, Khalti, IMEPay, PrabhuPay, and imply reduces the difficulty of this task[110]. There are now handful of wallet companies in Nepal of which twenty-six companies has already gained license from NRB.

In addition, banks are making an effort to encourage the usage of credit cards. The worldwide issue is that you are losing out on the tactile and tactile experience of purchasing things. As in other parts of the world, this is an issue in Nepal as well. An additional important problem for delivery is the lack of accurate street maps to guide the driver.

We started our own wallet company called UPay (or UnelmaPay.com. np)[111] however the government stopped issuing the license through a new monetary policy of NRB[112]. As a result, we had to stop the operation of digital wallet business in consultation with personnel from NRB. If you would ask my opinion Nepal government should not dictate licensing process and should allow any companies who are operating in Nepal to do

---

110 https://www.factopedianepal.com/list-of-best-digital-wallets-in-nepal/
111 https://unelmapay.com.np/
112 https://english.onlinekhabar.com/nepal-doubles-the-number-of-e-wallet-companies-in-8- months-but-most-of-them-face-sustainability-challenge.html

"recharge" business which is basically top-up of mobile phones operators. There is no need to distribute only limited license or stop the licensing in pressure of big market players. e-Sewa has the dominant market presence in Nepal for recharge business and representatives from that company dictate what NRB does in practice.

My research has shown a fascinating loop involving inadequate goods and consumer discontent. The operation of a large-scale internet shop in Nepal is a difficult and time-consuming endeavor. If someone from Kamal Binayak purchases something from one of the little businesses put up on Facebook, you can't just respond, "We're sorry, we can't transport your stuff there." For the first several years, online retailers must operate at a low-profit margin (if any) or even at the break-even threshold to continue business and build a brand identity. There is a compromise for this, just as there is for every other trade-off. Online businesses seem to overpromise or offer substandard items regularly to operate and compete in such a challenging climate.

Additionally, they do all they can to get visitors to purchase the goods. They must do it by presenting their goods in a visually appealing way. Customers would be disappointed when they get their orders since the items did not meet their expectations because the site portrayed the product in the most opulent manner possible, bragging about its features and quality. In Nepal, internet consumers have reported having a similar experience in the past. This unhappiness gave rise to the belief that "online purchasing is risky," and "they present one thing and deliver another." As a result, consumers lose trust in their ability to do online transactions and abandon online purchasing altogether. And so, it goes on in a circle.

12.4 The Importance of ecommerce in Development of Nepal

E-commerce is a massive business with millions of employees. It generated projected worldwide sales of more than 3.5 trillion dollars last year. This astonishing data suggests a shift in the global economy away from traditional trade and toward ecommerce. India and China are often recognized as the world's leading e-commerce markets, both in business development and the size of their respective consumer markets. Individual merchants and commercial companies have been allowed to deal via digital media due to their economic development and consumer market. In other words, the gap between consumers and enterprises has significantly shrunk in both India and China in recent years[113]. When it comes to a tiny economy like Nepal, local firms may profit from tapping into a huge number of the potential markets and commercial possibilities that foreign investors create. Additionally, considering consumer and cultural   commonalities, Nepali businesses may apply comparable e-commerce tactics tailored to their product and service offerings.

This implies that there are several e-commerce options available in the Nepali market today. Companies like Daraz and other e-commerce platforms have already begun to bridge the gap in trade between Nepali customers and Chinese and Indian firms. Bringing Nepali customers into the global market has opened the door to increased international commerce opportunities. There are administrative challenges to overcome but doing so would enable Nepali enterprises to compete on a global scale more effectively. Implementing digital commerce may allow firms to conduct trade on a standardized platform, altering the course of business in the future. Businesses are making every effort to make each customer's purchasing experience as personalized as possible.

Take-up of online commerce may assist organizations in achieving this specific aim by forecasting customer purchasing behavior and demands. Individual clients will have a unique experience depending on their geographical location, internet surfing history, previous behavior, and other factors. If you go to a retail purchasing site and type in "casual shirt," the e-commerce platform on the site would provide suggestions

---

113 Digitalisation and Development: Issues for India and Beyond.
https://link.springer.com/chap- ter/10.1007/978-981-13-9996-1_1

based on your previous internet surfing and online purchase history. In a similar vein, customers may get brands that have a customized brand value. Customers are influenced to make the proper purchase on e-commerce sites by providing relevant and useful material.

Chapter 13: The Food Industry in Nepal

The food processing and preservation sector has now evolved into something more akin to a need as opposed to a luxury. A significant contribution to the conservation and improved usage of food commodities produced in the nation is made by this organization. The use of contemporary ways to lengthen storage life for better distribution and processing procedures to preserve them for use in the off-season on both a big scale and a small scale is required to use the excess throughout the season, both in large-scale and small-scale operations. Furthermore, there has been significant growth in the degree of interest in food and agro-processing in recent years. Agro-processing and food processing have drawn the attention of planners and policymakers due to the potential contribution they have in advancing the country's economic growth. To improve the economic condition of the people in general and particularly impoverished segments of the nation, it is necessary to make better use of available resources, both material and human. Very little attention has been paid to the components of agricultural product handling, processing, and preservation, leading to their neglect. Multiple studies have shown that an estimated 40 percent of the overall output of agricultural commodities is tragically squandered due to insufficient processing facilities and a lack of post-harvest technological advancements.

Even though production is carried out in enormous quantities, processing has not yet been effectively established. Pre-processing of agricultural commodities occurs before they are suitable for use in ultimate conversion into processed foods, and it is included in the processing. Studies have demonstrated that high-value agricultural goods may successfully compete in both the local and worldwide markets, resulting in improved incomes for farmers and other disadvantaged groups due to their increased marketability. Fruits and vegetables are considered perishable commodities among agricultural commodities because they are available only during specific times of the year in different regions and are wasted in large quantities due to a lack of facilities, proper handling, distribution, marketing, and storage and because they are available only during specific times of the year in different regions.

Successful examples from adjacent countries illustrate that the formation of small commercial companies may enhance the living conditions of rural people, resulting in the growth of rural communities on both a social and an economic level. When it comes to business in Nepal; food, and geoprocessing firms are the sole viable option since they increase the nutritious value of food by eliminating hazardous chemicals, prolonging shelf life, and making it more appealing to consumers. These businesses can grow their market share, particularly if they enhance the quality of their products and provide more appealing packaging. Market strategies that are more aggressive are also required. Important aspects to examine include the availability of high-quality raw materials and if it is more cost-effective to create them locally rather than import them from other countries. Several potentially profitable Agro-product firms may be established in the county to capitalize on the available local resources of crops and horticulture products to alleviate poverty. It is possible to reduce poverty in the area as a whole via the proper use of food science and technology in food processing.

Such an application has the potential to mobilize local resources and produce a reliable source of revenue. A responsible role for the government of Nepal in mobilizing and organizing the country's agriculturalists is essential to attain this objective. Farmers from low-income groups in Nepal's villages should have access to modern technology to develop job opportunities. It is possible to improve people's socio-economic situation via the development of small-scale, locally based agricultural processing and marketing operations.

13.1 Impact of Food Sectors

In recent years, the market for cider, perry, and rice wine in Nepal was estimated to be worth sixteen million USD (measured in retail prices). The wine market in Nepal is expected to reach 40.41 million USD (in retail prices) by 2025, representing a compound annual growth rate (CAGR) of 9.22 percent for the period 2021-2025. This is a drop compared to the growth rate of around 11.80 percent per year recorded in 2020-2021. According to the World Bank, the average consumption per capita in value terms was 0.56 USD per capita (in retail prices) in 2021. It expanded at a compound annual growth rate (CAGR) of 10.34 percent each year during the following five years. In the long term (by 2025), the indicator is expected to reduce its development and expand at a compound annual growth rate (CAGR) of 7.38 percent per year.

Over the last several years, the worldwide cider, Perry, and rice wine markets have witnessed steady expansion, according to industry analysts. The category is heavily impacted by the increasing use of low-alcohol beverages throughout the globe, which is being driven by a shift in consumer lifestyle. Market participants are putting greater effort into the creation of artisan ciders while at the same time maintaining a strong emphasis on provenance and history. Furthermore, customers interested in living a better lifestyle are more likely to pay a premium for ciders that include a high concentration of juice. Another developing trend is the pairing of cider with food, which is anticipated to impact the product's place in the market. Over the last several years, China and the European area have dominated the global market in sales. The cider, Perry, and rice wine markets, particularly in Europe, were among the fastest expanding categories of alcoholic drinks in recent years. Furthermore, the area accounted for more than half of the global market consumption, with the United Kingdom as the leader. The desire for rosé cider is on the rise, as is the demand for Japanese rice wines, to name a few examples.

Sake is becoming more popular among sommeliers in the United Kingdom, seeking new and exciting products to give their customers. It is the purpose of this chapter to provide a strategic study of the Nepali cider, perry, and rice wines market, as well as a prognosis for its growth in the medium term, taking into consideration the influence of COVID-19 on the market. A complete analysis of the market's volume and value and the market's dynamics, segmentation, characteristics, major players, pricing, international trade, trends, insights into growth and demand drivers, as well as challenges is provided. This study is one of the most thorough available on the Nepali cider, perry, and rice wine markets, and it provides unrivaled value, accuracy, and professional insights in the process. Specifically, this chapter aims to provide accurate and expert-verified information regarding the volumes, values, dynamics, segmentation, and features of Nepali cider, perry, and rice wine consumption, as well as imports and exports of these beverages.

In addition, the chapter provides a projection for the market's growth in the near and medium-term, as well as an analysis of the influence COVID-19 has had and will continue to have on it. The chapter also includes a thorough examination of the major market players, industry trends and insights, growth and demand drivers and obstacles, and all other variables that influence the market's development. According to forecasts, the apple juice market in Nepal will reach 3.30 million USD (calculated at retail prices) by 2021. It is predicted that the juice market in Nepal will reach 8.71 million USD (in retail prices) by 2025, growing at a compound annual growth rate (CAGR) of 8.84 percent per year over the period 2021-2025. This is a drop compared to the growth rate of around 12.04 percent per year recorded in 2020-2021. In value terms, the average consumption per capita reached 0.12 USD per capita (in retail prices) in 2021, decreasing from 0.12 USD per capita in 2020. It expanded at a compound annual growth rate (CAGR) of 10.95 percent each year during the following five years. In the long term (by 2025), the indicator is expected to reduce its development and expand at a compound annual growth rate (CAGR) of 7.64 percent per year. People are drinking fewer but higher-quality juices these days, and they are ready to pay a higher price for the health advantages they believe they provide. As a result, the category of juices, particularly those containing 100 percent fruit, has increased in popularity among customers all over the globe. This is despite customer worry about the high sugar level of 100 percent apple juice, which has hindered the market's expansion in recent years because of health-conscious concerns about sugar consumption.

13.2 The First Step to Well-Developed Nepal

Due to improved levels of education, people are more easily able to grasp the key differences between artificial sugar and natural sugar, meaning they are more likely to view natural fruit juices more positively. In many countries, apple continues to be the second most popular taste after orange; however, younger customers are increasingly choosing more unique and unusual flavors such as celery, cucumber, beetroot, and other vegetables. Apple juice is the third most popular taste in most European nations. In the United States, apple juice is expected to account for around a-third of overall juice consumption in 2021. A further developing trend in the global juice industry is the widespread availability of cold-pressed juices. Their popularity may be attributed to a special processing method that is believed to retain better the taste of fruit juices and the micronutrients found in them, such as vitamins and minerals, than other methods.

Consumers are becoming more interested in homogenous juices, particularly in Europe, where most people prefer to drink juice manufactured from a single kind of fruit. In 2021, Nepal's market for other juices, juice combinations, and smoothies was estimated to be worth 22.80 million USD (measured in retail prices). The smoothie market in Nepal is expected to reach 57.27 million USD (in retail prices) by 2025, growing at a compound annual growth rate (CAGR) of 8.66 percent between 2021 and 2025. This is a drop compared to the growth rate of around 10.99 percent per year recorded in 2020-2021. In value terms, the average consumption per capita reached 0.80 USD per capita (in retail prices) in 2021, increasing from 0.70 USD per capita in 2020. It expanded at a compound annual growth rate (CAGR) of 9.91 percent each year during the following five years.

In the long term (by 2025), the indicator is expected to reduce its development and expand at a compound annual growth rate (CAGR) of 7.46 percent per year. People are drinking fewer but higher-quality juices these days, and they are ready to pay a higher price for the health advantages they believe they provide. As a result, the category of juices, particularly those containing 100 percent fruit, has increased in popularity among customers all over the globe

Their popularity may be attributed to a special processing method that is believed to cause the fruit juices to retain a better taste as well as their micronutrients, such as vitamins and minerals. Consumers are becoming more interested in homogenous juices, particularly in Europe, where most people historically preferred to drink juice manufactured from a single kind of fruit.

Nepal has opened the door to enormous development potential for market players in the information technology (IT) sector in recent years. This includes using new technology to expand and grow the online food industry and e-delivery services in the nation, which is one of the strategies being implemented. Using digital platforms that link farmers directly to end customers may actively benefit the national economy by encouraging development in the agriculture sector and contributing to overall economic growth. The newest food industry innovations, such as the cloud kitchen, require less upfront investment and are well suited for serving huge client groups throughout the nation. Innovative business models and industry convergence and increased Internet and smartphone usage are the primary drivers of development in this area. As part of its efforts to capitalize on the development potential in online meal delivery, the government should develop a variety of incentive programmers and favorable legislation. However, despite the growth drivers, obstacles such as a lack of adequate transportation infrastructure, difficulties in retaining employees, and a lack of knowledge among individuals in the suburbs limit the expansion of online food delivery platforms in Nepal.

Chapter 14: Healthcare in Nepal

Nepal continues to be one of the world's poorest nations and one that's most vulnerable to natural catastrophes, despite recent improvements. In addition, the nation is suffering from the consequences of climate change and population growth. Landslides and flash floods occur frequently, especially during the monsoon season. Every year, more than five hundred people are killed in these disasters. Medical treatment in the nation is often unequally distributed, with most of the country's healthcare resources concentrating in and around the country's main metropolitan areas. The inequitable allocation of resources harms the quality and accessibility of healthcare in Nepal. The Alma Ata Declaration of 1978 stressed the need for preventative, promotional, and curative healthcare services centered in the community. By building a network of basic healthcare institutions, Nepal has also made strides toward improving the quality of life for its population. In addition, the nation sent community healthcare workers to deliver healthcare at the grassroots level in communities around the country[114]. In Nepal, the improvement in healthcare has resulted in a significant rise in the average life expectancy. According to the Nepali Times, from 1991 and 2021, the average life expectancy increased by 12.3 years.

---

114 About Race, Poverty and the Environment.
   https://www.reimaginerpe.org/book/export/ html/372

Current life expectancy in Bangladesh is the second highest in South Asia, partly due to the country's dramatic decline in infant mortality rates over the last decade. When the Central Bureau of Statistics published its figures in 2018, it said that 2,95, 4,59 Nepalis were above seventy-five percent. By 2021, the figure had climbed to 437, 981. In rural regions, the death rate for children under five declined from 1,43 per 10,00 to 50 per 1000 live births in 2020[115].

The vast majority of Nepal's healthcare resources are concentrated in or around Kathmandu, the country's capital city. As a result of this concentration, various parts of Nepal are being ignored. On the other hand, Nepal's government established a Social Health Insurance Development Committee as a legislative framework in an attempt to begin establishing a social health security plan in the country. Increasing access to healthcare services for Nepal's impoverished and disadvantaged groups was one of the program's primary objectives. It was also intended to improve accessibility for individuals who reside in remote or difficult- to-reach sections. The finance of the project, however, continues to provide difficulties. In its Interim Constitution, the Nepalese government recognized healthcare as a fundamental human right. Despite their efforts, only 61.8 percent of Nepalese have access to healthcare services within a thirty-minute driving distance. Nepal is also plagued by an insufficient supply of key pharmaceuticals and a lack of oversight over private healthcare practitioners. Nepal also has a low number of physicians and nurses per 1,000 population, according to statistics. According to the World Health Organization, 2.3 physicians, nurses, and midwives should be assigned to every 1,000 people.

According to government estimates, around 22 percent of Nepalis do not have access to basic healthcare services. The Dalits from the Terai region and Muslims are the most common groups in Nepal who do not

---

115 10 Facts About Healthcare in Nepal - The Borgen Project.
https://borgenproject.org/health- care-in-nepal/

have access to healthcare. On the other hand, outpatient care has seen a 19 percent rise in the number of Dalits who seek it.

The following are the most common illnesses in Nepal: Ischemic heart disease, chronic obstructive pulmonary disease (COPD), lower respiratory infection, diarrhoeal illness, stroke, and diabetes. More than half of Nepalese adults suffer from bacterial tooth decay, according to the World Health Organization. Bacterial tooth decay may result in persistent pain, heart disease, or diabetes. Many people in remote communities may not have access to dental fillings, toothpaste, or even clean water to drink. Some Nepalese believe that tooth extraction would result in blindness if teeth were removed too soon.

The earthquakes that struck Nepal in April of 2015 were one of the most devastating natural catastrophes in the country's modern history, demolishing more than 1,100 healthcare institutions in the process. PossibleHealth.org, a global team of people dedicated to the belief that everyone deserves access to high-quality healthcare without financial hardship, signed a ten-year agreement with their government partners to attempt to rebuild the healthcare system in the Doodah district, which had 85 percent of its healthcare facilities destroyed by the earthquake.

According to the Himalayan Times, although attempts are being made to better the life of Nepalis, corruption abounds inside the government. Nepal is ranked one hundred seventeen out of one hundred and seventy- five nations in the world, according to the Corruption Perceptions Index[116]. As a result of this corruption, there are insufficient resources allocated to healthcare. The Nepalese government devotes just 5 percent of the national budget to healthcare, which is insufficient to bring about major advances.

Compared to other nations in South Asia, Nepal has made very modest strides in expanding access to health insurance coverage. Despite

---

116 https://thehimalayantimes.com/kathmandu/transparency-international-
places-ne- pal-at-117-in-corruption-perceptions-index

a lengthy history of the introduction of health insurance (HI) and the government of Nepal placing a high emphasis on the issue, the country has not been able to expand its social health insurance coverage to the vast majority of its people[117]. There are several obstacles to overcome to obtain universal health coverage in Nepal, ranging from policy stagnation to programmed implementation. The purpose of this research is to determine the Enrolment and drop out rates of health insurance and the factors that influence these rates in selected districts of Nepal. The research was carried out utilizing a mixed-method approach that included quantitative and qualitative data collection techniques. Nepal's Health Insurance Board (HIB) provided the numerical data on enrolment and drop out rates for this study.

Three districts in Nepal, namely Bardiya, Chitwan, and Gorkha, were specifically chosen for the qualitative data collection. Participants in the research were recruited from the Enrolment assistants (EA) ranks for the social health insurance program. Focus group discussions (FGDs) were held with the chosen EAs under the guidance of certain guidelines and unstructured interview questions. Using numerical data and focus group talks, the findings were synthesized and presented in the appropriate format. The outcomes of the research indicated that there was a wide range in enrolment and drop out rates in health insurance among the districts.

The reluctant participants who dropped out came from various socioeconomic backgrounds, including relatively well-off families, government workers, company owners, migrants, certain local political figures, and families from lower-middle and lower-income classes. Unavailability of sufficient drugs, unfriendly behavior of health workers, and indifferent behavior of care personnel toward insured patients in health care facilities were the most significant determinants of poor Enrolment

117 Status and determinants of Enrolment and drop out of health insurance, https://resource-allo- cation.biomedcentral.com/articles/10.1186/s12962-020-00227-7

and drop out, with insured patients preferring to receive health services in private clinics for their benefits. Several problems were contributing to inefficient programmed and policy implementation, including a lengthy maturation period before health services could be activated, a restricted health package, and a lack of copayment in many forms of health care. The high rate of drop outs and subsidized membership, which is a major problem for Nepal's health insurance program's long-term viability, is a major source of concern. Increased Enrolment and decreased drop out rates may be achieved by revising the current HI policy on health care packages, providing additional copayment options, increasing the capacity of Enrolment assistants, and improving cooperation between the health insurance board and health care institutions.

Chapter 15: The Schools of Nepal

Nepal has become a more prominent sending country for international students in recent years. When compared to the previous year, the number of Nepali students in the United States[118] rose by more than 20 percent, the fastest growth rate among the top twenty-five sending nations by far. In this way, Nepal has managed to avoid the "Trump impact," which resulted in a general fall in new foreign student Enrolments. One of the causes contributing to the departure of Nepali students is the lack of educational and job possibilities in the country. A combination of political instability – there have been nine different administrations alone – and severe earthquakes in 2015 have exacerbated the country's socioeconomic circumstances. Although the government strives to enhance the education system via changes such as expanding obligatory basic education to eight years of schooling, the education system continues to face challenges. Nepal is a tiny nation with a population of twenty-nine million people located at the top of the planet.

Nepal, tucked between the mega-countries of China and India, is home to eight of the world's ten tallest mountains, including Mount Everest, which is the highest peak on the planet. Nepal's mountainous geography,

---

118 How many Nepali students are in the USA? - Mero Kalam.
   https://www.merokalam.com/ nepali-students-in-america/

which renders it a landlocked nation, provides enormous hurdles for socioeconomic growth and makes it difficult and expensive to upgrade and extend the country's infrastructure. Nepal's earthquake vulnerability is another factor hindering the country's socio-economic progress. In 2015, the nation was attacked by two successive earthquakes, one of which was the strongest to hit the country in more than eight decades. More than 8,600 people died due to this terrible disaster, which also destroyed or badly damaged major portions of the country's infrastructure, including almost 500,000 homes and more than 9,300 public schools. In the aftermath of the disaster, hundreds of thousands of families were uprooted, and more than 700,000 people were forced into poverty. The consequences for the school system were catastrophic, and the process of rehabilitation is taking its time. One year after the earthquake, more than 70 percent of those displaced from their homes in the worst-hit districts were still living in temporary shelters.

Many students were forced to attend school in homemade tents, which resulted in a significant rise in drop outs and grade repetitions. As of recent times, just 88,112 private residences and 2,891 schools have been renovated since the beginning of the century. The high level of political instability and fragmentation in Nepal is one of the factors contributing to the country's poor recovery development. Nepali society is still dominated by agriculture and is extremely stratified, with upper- caste Hindu rulers ruling over a heterogeneous community that comprises 125 ethnic groups/castes and speaks 123 different languages (according to the latest 2021 census). It is estimated that just 44.6 percent of the population speaks Nepali, its official language, as their first language. Even though Hindus account for 81.3 percent of the population, there are significant caste differences within the Hindu community. Reduced social mobility and deprivation of lower-caste people, particularly Dalits ("untouchables") and other religious minorities (10 percent and 4 percent of the population, respectively), has been a cause of strife in

India for decades. Lower castes and other oppressed groups have less access to basic amenities and education and fewer prospects for social progress than their upper-caste counterparts. A similar pattern may be seen in Nepal, marked by significant regional inequalities and urban-rural divisions between more developed areas such as the Kathmandu Valley and less developed rural parts. The country of Nepal has seen a violent Maoist insurgency that lasted for ten years, as well as the brief restoration of the absolute monarchy after a royal coup d'état in 2018. The signing of a peace accord set the stage for the ultimate re-democratization of Nepal's political system, culminating in the country's first parliamentary elections in 17 years.

Meanwhile, it remains to be seen if parliamentary elections and the adoption of a federal and more inclusive constitution[119] would be able to stop the tide of political instability and volatility now afflicting Nepal. The political process continues to be marked by infighting and corruption among the participants. Violence followed the approval of the new constitution and the run-up to the parliamentary elections which took place in the same year. However, although political instability has hampered progress on many fronts so far, most analysts think that federalism is the best form of administration for a nation with such a varied ethnic and religious population and a divided political system as Nepal. The development of the political system is also considered to have had a role in promoting educational changes. Additionally, despite political turbulence and natural disasters, the Nepali economy continues to expand at a healthy pace.

The absence of top-tier colleges, scholarships, and post-graduate job possibilities in Nepal's developing economy reduces the country's appeal as a study destination for international students from other parts of the world. Nepal does not rely on neighboring nations as a source of students; neither India nor China provide a large number of them. In Nepal in 2021,

119 Education in Nepal - WENR. https://wenr.wes.org/2018/04/education-in-nepal

the only year for which data is available from the UNESCO Institute of Statistics (UIS), there were 107 foreign degree students. According to the Institute of International Education (IIE), 370 students from the United States were studying in Nepal in 2021 (Open Doors). However, outbound mobility is on the rise: between 2020 and 2021, the number of Nepali students enrolled in degree programmers overseas increased by 835 percent, reaching 44,255 students at the end of the decade (UIS). Moreover, while this number is lower than the number of international students from major Asian sending countries such as the People's Republic of China, India, or Vietnam, it should be noted that the outbound mobility ratio in Nepal – that is, the proportion of international students among all students – is significantly higher in Nepal than in these major Asian sending countries. Over the previous decade, Nepal's outward mobility ratio has almost doubled, and it is currently more than twelve times higher than that of its neighboring country, India.

According to the World Bank, Nepal's mobility ratio in 2021 was 12.3 percent, but it was 0.9 percent, 1.9 percent, and 3 percent in India, China, and Vietnam, respectively. It is hardly unexpected that Nepali students are becoming more mobile in their studies. Since Nepal is a country in constant flux, a significant rise in international student mobility has coincided with a significant increase in labor migration from Nepal during the past decade. According to official figures, as much as 28 percent of Nepal's labor force (four million out of fourteen million employees) is presently employed abroad. Many overseas students are departing Nepal in the same way as these employees, citing a lack of higher education alternatives, rising unemployment among young people, and the chance of better education and career possibilities abroad. Soon, it is expected that the number of Nepalese students who go abroad will expand even more. By 2031, the country's population is expected to have increased from 29 million to 33.6 million people, reflecting the country's increasing affluence and population growth. Nepal is now going through a "youth bulge period" in terms of population: the country has many young people. According to World Bank data, the proportion of university-age youths in the Nepali population (ages 20 to 29) was approximately 36 percent in 2021, and analysts predict that Nepal will be one of the countries with the fastest-growing population of eighteen to twenty-two--year-olds in the coming years. The youth population rise will raise demand for education and place greater pressure on the educational system. According to the ICEF Monitor, the situation in Nepal is similar to that of other South Asian nations, where the demand for education is fast, outstripping the availability of educational opportunities. According to projections, graduate-level mobility will increase, in particular in Nepal, which has a developing sector with fewer than one percent of university campuses providing doctoral programmers.

According to a recent report by the British Council, Nepal would be one of the top ten nations with the fastest growth rates in outward mobility over the next decade, with countries such as China, India, Pakistan, and Nigeria, among others. Approximately 20,000 more overseas Nepali students are expected to enroll by 2027, according to the Nepali Students' Advisory Council. Nepali students study abroad in countries such as Australia, India, the United States, Japan, and the United Kingdom, which is the most popular destinations for Nepali students. Nepal has become the third-largest sending country for international students in Australia, following China and India during the previous several years. Following figures given by the Australian Government Department of Education and Training, Nepal accounted for 5 percent of the 621,192 international students in Australia as of November 2021. This could be due to a significant number of top-quality colleges, simplified visa requirements. Comparatively, affordable expenses of education when compared to countries such as the United States and the United Kingdom, Australia is almost certain to remain a popular study destination for Nepalese students in the future. Also, in the United States, the number of Nepalese students has risen dramatically in the last two years.

Nepal is presently the 13th most popular place of origin with 11,607 students. Engineers and math/computer science majors are the most popular choices among Nepali students, with physical/life sciences and mathematics/computer science following closely after. Because STEM education is still undeveloped in Nepal, and graduates in technical subjects have better work opportunities when they return home, STEM degrees will probably continue to be popular among young people. Currently, the majority of Nepalese students in the United States are enrolled at the undergraduate level (54 percent), where recent Enrolment growth has been the most significant (34.4 percent were enrolled in graduate programmers, with the remainder enrolled in other programmers in the academic year 2021).

While Nepal is an interesting and emerging recruiting market for U.S. colleges, Nepali students are hindered by a lack of financial resources. They would benefit immensely from targeted scholarship programmers, which are now lacking. Many Nepali students in areas such as New York and California are said to work long hours in odd occupations to fund their education there. Although the nation saw several political defeats over the following decades, the current Nepali education system did not emerge until 1951, when the country transitioned from an absolute monarchy to a more representative political structure. Education was still considered a luxury reserved for the upper classes in Nepal in the 1950s, with about 5 percent of the population being literate and around 10,000 pupils enrolled in only a few hundred schools (less than 1 percent of the population). When the nation lacked access to higher education, In Nepal's strict Hindu-dominated culture, women were discriminated against and discouraged from entering school. In the years afterward, education has become much more widely available and affordable for more people. Modern education reforms, such as the 1971 National Education System Plan, have resulted in a considerably more modern and equal education system, with obligatory public basic education as the foundation. The number of primary and secondary schools in Nepal have increased to 35,222. The country now has ten universities with more than 1,400 institutions and campuses spread around the country, according to the latest figures (2021). Nepal's government considers expanding educational opportunities to be a top priority, and its current 2021 School Sector Development Plan aims to remove the nation from the category of "least developed country" by 2022 "through improving ... access and quality of education." There has been significant improvement. Nowadays, most Nepali youngsters have far greater educational chances than their parents had while they were growing up. According to the U.S. Department of Education data[120], net Enrolment rates in primary education climbed from 66.3 to 97 percent between 2020 and 2021 (World Bank). Following an increase from 44.9 percent in 2020 to 60.4 percent in 2021, net enrolment rates in secondary school dropped to 54.4 percent in 2021, most likely due to the earthquake that occurred in Japan in 2021. Increasing female involvement in school has seen the most significant benefits. Over thirty years, the gender parity index for school Enrolments in elementary and secondary education increased from 0.17 to 1.08, indicating that female admission rates into education have improved from being marginal at best to females currently enrolling at somewhat greater rates than boys (World Bank).

A high drop out rate remains a problem in the educational system, with females being more prone than boys to abandon their studies early. Despite significant increases in retention rates over the previous few decades, only 76.8 percent of students in cohorts that begin in primary education will make it to the end of the elementary school system by the year 2021 (UNESCO). Most young people who drop out of school are from low-income families or reside a long distance away from their

---

120 According to the U.S Department of Education, University, https://ttlc.intuit.com/commu- nity/college-education/discussion/according-to-the-u-s-department-of-education-universi- ty/01/73873

schools. Because they must assist their parents with agricultural chores or travel great distances to attend school, children from impoverished homes are sometimes compelled to drop out. In addition, education for girls is still not seen as a high priority in some rural homes, and child marriage is still a reasonably widespread practice, even in urban areas. "Three-quarters of Nepal's girls marry before the age of eighteen, and ten percent are married before the age of fifteen," according to Human Rights Watch. Generally speaking, completion rates in Nepal's school system decrease with increasing levels of education: according to the most recent UNESCO statistics, the completion rate in lower-secondary education stands at 69.7 percent in 2021 and drops dramatically to 24.5 percent at the upper-secondary level (2021).

Lower castes and other impoverished groups continue to be underrepresented in the educational system, and their drop out rates continue to be higher. For example, just 23.1 percent of Dalits were literate in 2021 in the Terai region, which is on the border with India, compared to 80 percent of the upper castes such as Brahmans and Chhetri's in the same area. The overall adult literacy rate in the nation remains alarmingly low, standing at just 60 percent in 2021, far lower than the worldwide average of 84.6 percent at the time of the census (the youth literacy rate was much higher at 84.8 percent, but still below the global average of 89.6 percent in the same year). In 2021, just 56 percent of the Nepali population over the age of twenty-five had completed higher education than a lower secondary level. It shows itself in the country's very low tertiary, gross enrolment ratio of 14.9 percent in 2021, which is less than half the worldwide average and 12 percentage points lower than the Enrolment rate in its neighboring India at the same time. A shift is taking place in Nepal's political system.

As a result of the constitution, Nepal has been divided into seven distinct states, with governmental authority, including education administration, projected to be further devolved to the states and local authorities. Although there have been some successes, the implementation of the new federal system has been a tumultuous and slow-moving process that failures have beset. In this transition period, not all local governments are fully operational, and much of Nepal's education system continues to be administered under the previous system, in which the Ministry of Education oversaw five Regional Educational Directorates, under which there were various District Education Offices and Resource Centers tasked with implementing policies at the grassroots level. For the whole nation, the Federal Ministry of Education (MOE) creates comprehensive educational policies and directives. In the federal system, it is unclear how exactly the Ministry of Education's role will evolve. However, the MOE's responsibilities continue to be inclusive curriculum and textbook development, teacher training, teacher recruitment, and conceptualizing and administering Nepal's national school-leaving examinations through its National Education Board. The University Grants Commission (UGC) is a regulatory organization under the jurisdiction of the Ministry of Education that oversees universities across the country.

The national curriculum framework, which is presently under revision, establishes the fundamentals of elementary and secondary education programmers. For example, language instruction (both Nepali and mother languages), English, mathematics, sciences (including social sciences), physical education, and several optional topics in upper grades are included under this umbrella subject area of education. Promotion is determined by end-of-term and end-of-year school tests, while the eighth grade is concluded with a district-wide final examination in which all students participate. From April, the academic year is based around Nepali New Year.

A calendar based on the Bikram Sambat system is used in Nepal, which differs from the Roman calendar in many ways (the year 2021 is the year 2077 in Nepal). Nepali is the language of instruction in public schools, although English is the language of teaching in many private institutions. It is stipulated in Nepal's current "school sector development plan" that minority languages should be employed as the major medium of teaching in grades one to three in places where these languages are the lingua franca to improve educational achievements for underprivileged students. This adjustment has been implemented to make it simpler for students who do not speak Nepali at home to understand the school curriculum. Although the reforms are making headway, the shortage of qualified instructors and instructional materials in these languages has slowed the pace of change.

Preceding the most recent changes, the secondary school system was separated into two years of lower secondary education (grades nine and ten) and two years of higher secondary education (grades eleven and twelve). Each segment was culled in its national examination. Both levels have been integrated into a single four-year secondary school cycle under the present system. After being renamed "Secondary Education Examination," the original national School Leaving Certificate (SLC) Examination, which was conducted at the end of grade ten, will now be held at the regional level (SEE). There will be just one final national school-leaving test administered after grade twelve, which will be administered nationwide. These reforms have been in the works for quite some time, but they were finally signed into law and are presently being implemented. Passing the final district-level test at the end of grade eight is required for admission to secondary school programmers. General secondary courses and vocational-technical secondary tracks are available to students to pursue their educational goals.

Mandatory courses such as Nepali, English, Physics, Mathematics, and Social Sciences are included in the general curriculum, as well as a vocationally focused topic, and one optional subject. The general curriculum includes a compulsory subject like mathematics (in addition to a local language, foreign language, or another vocational subject). Vocational/technical streams, on the other hand, have a more applied emphasis in subject areas such as agriculture, medicine, forestry, and engineering. Although still in the early stages of development, this stream is currently only available at a small number of institutions around the country. To better prepare graduates for work, according to the recent education law, students pursuing a vocational route will henceforth be obliged to take an extra one-year practical course after completing grade twelve. Examinations throughout the year and a final test after the year serve as the basis for assessment and advancement. Students under the former system had to pass the difficult national SLC examinations at the end of grade ten to higher secondary school. These tests were dubbed the "iron gate" because of the very low pass rates in the exams (less than 48 percent of candidates passed). While the system is still in flux, it seems likely that the (perhaps less rigorous) region-level SEE tests at the end of grade 10 will continue to be necessary for promotion to grade eleven in the future.

The National Examinations Board performs final examinations in secondary school and holds an external national examination every three years (previously the Higher Secondary Education Board). It is now known as the National Examination Board Examination Certificate, and it is issued to candidates who complete the examination (previously the Higher Secondary Education Board Examination Certificate). Alternatively, students can enroll in university-preparatory programs offered by universities that lead to a "Proficiency Certificate," a credential that allows them to continue their education beyond high school[121] (a similar type of credential may be referred to as an "Intermediate Certificate" at some institutions). Admission to Proficiency Certificate programmers may be contingent on passing an entrance test. Programs typically last two or three years and include general education with

---

121 Johnson, Carrie, et al. "What Are Student Loan Borrowers Thinking? Insights From Focus Groups on College Selection and Student Loan Decision Making." Journal of Financial Counseling and Planning, vol. 27, no. 2, Association for Financial Counseling and Planning Education, July 2016, p. 184.

specialized studies. This kind of curriculum is gradually being phased away, although it is still available at certain colleges and universities. The National Test Board examination is now transitioning from a numerical grading scale to a letter grade system with nine grades (A+, A, B+, B, C+, C, D, E, and N). Nevertheless, the percentage-based grading system described below was still in operation: Generally speaking, secondary education in Nepal is carried out at so-called community schools, which are public institutions that the government either entirely or mostly support.

While private schools, sometimes known as "institutional schools," are gaining popularity, they remain a tiny proportion of the overall student population. The number of community schools in Nepal was 29,207, including 6,015 private secondary schools. Private school Enrolments accounted for 17.2 percent of all Enrolments at the lower-secondary level. Privately sponsored private schools often provide higher-quality education. In the SLC tests, for example, private school students achieve far better pass rates than public school students, which were at about 90 percent earlier, compared to just 34 percent for public school students at the same time. The majority of Nepalis cannot afford private schooling. Nevertheless, even studying at public institutions is out of the reach of many low-income families, which has a detrimental impact on participation rates in educational opportunities overall.

There are no requirements for secondary education in Nepal, nor is it completely free. Women, ethnic minorities, and children from low-income families are all guaranteed the right to "free education up to the secondary level from the state," according to the current constitution, which follows the previous interim constitution. Realistically, however, many parents are still expected to pay school fees and cover the costs of other goods such as textbooks, instructional materials, and uniforms. Even in recent times, individual families continued to bear more than half of all expenses on secondary education in Nepal. Religious schools (Madrasas, Ashrams, and so on) that teach the national school curriculum are available in the community. Several international schools in Nepal provide a foreign curriculum in addition to the native ones. For example, the British School in Kathmandu follows the British curriculum and prepares pupils for British certifications such as the International Certificate of General Secondary Education (IGCSE).

The most effective tool for development is education. One of the main issues in both developed and emerging nations is the caliber of education. The majority of nations do not adequately spend resources to address this issue, which has an impact on our children's futures. The standard of education is determined by a number of elements, but the quality is only one of them.

The Nepalese government makes it a priority to raise educational standards and promote skill development. Since it is a fundamental human right, the Nepalese government has proudly fought to promote education. It carries out responsibilities ranging from primary school work through programs at the higher secondary and graduation level.

Nowadays, there are many public and private colleges available in Nepal for Higher education. However, many Indian, as well as foreign students, frequently travel to Tribhuvan University and Kathmandu University for their academic needs[122]. Each student works hard to further their education and achieve the quality they seek. Educational institutions in Nepal made significant efforts to repair and raise the standard of the equation. However, compared to public institutions, private colleges in Nepal are significantly more furnished and equipped.

Chapter 16: Nepal: A Failing State or A Transitional State?

As a result of my study, I have discovered that some groups and castes are offered little to no opportunity to work in the public sector in Nepal. Castes from lower social strata, women from lower socioeconomic strata, and the impoverished continue to be among the most vulnerable in our society, with limited access to civic institutions and resources. Education is also unequally distributed, with Madhesh constituting seven out of ten of Nepal's least educated districts, with an average literacy rate of 48.77 percent in these seven districts.

Furthermore, the average income in these regions is far lower than the national average, and it is still fairly typical for Madhesi females to drop out of school before completing their secondary education. When it comes to demonstrating their abilities based on merit and achievements, those born into the privilege of a family name, business connections, and inherited wealth have a distinct advantage over those who are not. Those who are not born into these advantages are simply not evaluated or considered. There are a variety of societal challenges that influence our nation on a day-to-day basis. Many people have very diverse perspectives on these issues, providing a variety of ways to resolve them and a variety of hypotheses as to why they arise.

However, due to the unpredictable nature of the frequency and manner of occurrence of these social concerns, they cannot be eliminated. They must instead be confined to be managed. Trying new things and listening to everyone's opinions, not just those who agree with us, are the only ways we can improve these circumstances, if not eliminate them. We can still tackle the problem by offering technical education to youngsters, developing factories and businesses, and reforming our traditional agricultural and cottage industries, all while ensuring that laws and regulations are strictly adhered to and enforced. Nepal is considered to be one of the world's least developed nations. Several social difficulties and evils exist in today's society. Social difficulties and evils are issues that have an impact on the people who live in a society. It is customary to use the phrase "social issue" to describe difficulties that affect a certain region or group of people across the globe.

Alcoholism, racism, child abuse, and other social ills also influences the way individuals respond to specific events. Nepal is confronted with many societal issues, including the caste system, child labor, illiteracy, gender inequality, superstitions, religious disputes, and a slew of other issues. The decision of a couple to abort a newborn girl is one of the most visible manifestations of gender prejudice in our culture. In Nepal, caste discrimination was the primary cause of the country's "civil war." The usage of alcoholic beverages, smoking, and drug addiction are ravaging the country's adolescent population. Some of them are completely unaware of the consequences of their actions. Child abuse also occurs, and it may take many forms, including physical, sexual, and emotional. The majority of mistreated children suffer more mental harm than physical harm.

One individual is not accountable for the issues that exist in society today. It is past time to put an end to these heinous societal ills that plague us. Illiteracy and poverty are also key contributors to the emergence of societal ills. Social difficulties and evils are the primary impediments to

Why Nepal Fails 201

the development of society. Approximately 27 percent of the population lives in absolute poverty. Living standards in rural regions are low as a result of slow expansion in the agriculture industry. This contributes to poverty in rural communities. The increasing population has placed a significant strain on available agricultural land.

Superstitious ideas, which are strongly ingrained in Nepalese society, also contribute to the escalation of societal issues. Traditional beliefs can sometimes hold people back from moving forward in life. This occurs as a result of the innocence of the participants. Untouchability was made illegal in the year 2020 BS, yet it remains deeply ingrained to this day. In the mountainous region of the far western region, the Deuki system is one of the wicked social practices, traditions, or cultures. In this system, impoverished people sacrifice their young daughters to the gods.

The practice of giving cash or gifts to the bridegroom from the bride's father at the wedding ceremony is known as the dowry system. There is a widespread idea that adult females should not live at the family home for an excessive amount of time, leading to their marriage at a young age. This can trigger mental and physical issues that can ultimately result in maternal deaths before or during childbirth. In Nepal, many people still regard women to be inferior to males in terms of strength. Many still believe that women were designed to be servants to their male counterparts. Daughters are still treated as though they are commodity that can be exchanged between individuals. Many individuals still feel that females should not be allowed to go to school.

16.1 How Nepal Can Succeed

A protracted political shift in Nepal has slowed the growth of the banking sector, a crucial component of the nation's economic expansion. The sector controls the flow of funding from public, private, and international sources to enterprises, infrastructure, and development projects in both rural and urban regions; opening it up might considerably boost entrepreneurship and foreign investment and give a boost to sustainable economic growth.

In Nepal, a large number of individuals lack simple access to financial services. The World Bank, the Asian Development Bank, the International Finance Corporation (IFC), and other financial institutions have been actively assisting Nepal's central bank and other financial institutions to not only strengthen the financial system but also bring financial services to the largely unbanked population. Development agencies like the Department for International Development (DFID) and USAID have also been actively involved in this effort. But development has been slow.

Nepal is often regarded as the only low-income nation to have achieved significant strides in recent decades in poverty reduction, public health, and educational attainment. But will these accomplishments be able to be maintained during this 2020-2030 decade?

Between 1996 and 2016, the country's maternal mortality rate dropped from 539 deaths per 100,000 live births to 239 deaths per 100,000 live births. In only two decades, the adult literacy rate increased from 20 percent in the 1980s to 67 percent in 2018, while Nepalis living below the poverty line decreased from 42 percent to 21 percent. Despite this, the poorest people continue to lack access to inexpensive healthcare. The drop out rate from school is almost as high as the enrolling rate. Those who live in metropolitan areas breathe some of the most polluted air on the planet, which may reduce their life expectancy by up to four years. Many people do not have access to clean drinking water. It was hoped that local elections in 2017, held after a 20-year hiatus, would eliminate these gaps by producing responsible, elected authorities. The enthusiasm has waned two years after it first appeared. The current status of the state stays unchanged. Deputy National Planning Commission Chairman Min Bahadur Shahi believes the elections, *"helped us establish grassroots democracy and decentralize power,"* but *"the absence of accountability at all levels of government continues to be a big concern"* (NPC). *"As a result, the principal priority of the National People's Congress's 15th periodic plan is governance reform, corruption control, and transparency promotion.*"

As we enter the next decade, there are concerns regarding Nepal's progress in human development, particularly whether the country is on target to reach the United Nations' Sustainable Development Goals (SDGs) and achieve double-digit growth in the coming years. To achieve these goals, significant expenditures in healthcare, education, and nutrition will be required. As a result of noncommunicable illnesses, Nepal is now burdened by a double burden: growing rates of diabetes, cardiovascular disease, and cancer, all of which are costly to treat, while the poor continue to die from infections that are readily cured.

"Our efforts now should be focused on strengthening primary health care and prevention and early detection of diseases using existing tools, as well as new technologies such as artificial intelligence for virtual expert consultation and drug delivery," said Sanjib Sharma, a doctor at the BP Koirala Institute for Health Sciences in Dharan. According to the World Health Organization, despite a reduction in poverty by half, one-third of Nepali children are still malnourished. Women's anemia has grown in recent years, which is a worrying trend. Since its inception in 2012, the government's Multi-sectoral Nutrition Plan has worked hard to promote maternal and child health while increasing immunization rates and reducing child malnutrition. According to Kiran Rupakhetee of the Nepal Planning Commission, *"Development in Nepal is still associated with roads, but investing in early childhood development is equally vital; it is a development component."* The NPC wants nutrition programs to reach the most remote areas of the country.

Even as literacy rates climb, gender imbalance is anticipated to persist in the following decade, despite improvements in education. As female literacy increases, for example, the rates of child marriage and girls' drop out will continue to rise. According to experts, enhancing the quality of teaching at community schools, encouraging female students to pursue technical careers, and boosting applied education should be top priorities in the next ten years. Although Nepal is predicted to transition from the lower-middle-income nation classification by 2030, achieving the Sustainable Development Goals (SDGs) will be difficult. This will need the expenditure of $1 billion each year by the government only on infrastructure. Nepal aspires to attain double-digit growth of more than 10 percent during the next decade and a per capita income of $1,595 by the end of this decade.

According to Ms. Joshi, a gender and development specialist, said, "*I am optimistic about our possibilities.*" However, she believes that if we improve the economic condition of women, who account for more than half of the population, we will get there sooner. According to a World Bank analysis published in 2020, however, Nepal will fall short of its middle-income objective if current trends continue. It noted that, despite significant reductions in poverty rates, the country's development route has not resulted in economic growth but has instead created a scarcity of employment at home, which is fueling additional outmigration. Furthermore, although remittances account for one-third of the country's gross domestic product (GDP), they are a symptom of deeper-rooted, longer-lasting issues.

In the next ten years, there will be a wave of new hydropower and huge infrastructure projects, a surge in tourism and the service industry, and greater transportation and communication, according to planners, which will encourage young people to stay at home rather than seek work abroad.

"We recognize that our goals are lofty, but we also recognize that we are operating in the most favorable climate possible. The economy has reached a point of stability; current growth is already at 7 percent, several important hydropower projects are getting underway, and we have made significant investments in information technology," Supachai said.

"The decade of the 2020s will be a progressive decade of sustainable and fair development," Shahi predicts with optimism. "There will be affluence as well as social justice in the world. There will be double-digit growth, as well as greater government investment, and the emphasis will be on quality rather than quantity."

16.2 Steps to Help Nepal Succeed

As said by Kenneth J. Arrow in praise for book in "Why Nations Fail" that "The openness of a society, its willingness to permit creative destruction, and the rule of law appear to be decisive for economic development." Nepal should make full use of the resources that are available. Its primary responsibility is to ensure peace and security in the nation. Nepal should aim to create a greater quantity of hydroelectricity from its fast-flowing rivers since it is anticipated that the country will generate up to 83000 megawatts of energy. In Nepal, as we all know, there are several problems such as illiteracy, poverty, superstition, unemployment, brain drain, prejudice, traditional thinking, and a host of other issues. Nepal should address all of these issues and make every effort to find solutions to all of them. The leader of Nepal should be truthful and highly educated, and the residents of Nepal should be free to pick the best representation for them since the majority of Nepalese politicians are corrupt in some capacity. Given the fact that Nepal is a nation of natural beauty, many visitors used to travel from all over the globe to view and enjoy the magnificent landscape, historical palaces, religious places, and a variety of other attractions. As a result, Nepal should strive to improve in these areas while simultaneously expanding its trade with other nations. Nepal should strive to become more and more self-sufficient while simultaneously attempting to export as much as feasible and import as little as possible of the product. Besides these, there are other additional areas in which Nepal might be improved.

Two basic guidelines should guide the growth of Nepal's financial sector based on world economic forum suggestions[123]:

---

123 https://www.weforum.org/agenda/2015/01/2-ways-to-revamp-nepals-economy/

16.2.1 Develop the banking system

The central bank has brought out guidelines pushing banks and financial institutions to boost their capital base, which has contributed to a good trend in mergers, acquisitions, and the general strengthening of the balance sheets. Institutions may benefit from this shift by operating their urban operations more effectively and expanding their capacity to open branches in far-flung locations.

While this is going on, institutions may reach unbanked communities by utilizing technological solutions like mobile banking. It's thought that 80 percent of people now use mobile devices, which might be important. There are a few firms in Nepal, such as Finaccess and MNepal, that are building systems that allow banks to communicate with clients. In addition to bringing in deposits that were previously absent from the banking system, the development of mobile bank accounts also facilitates the expansion of a company's credit portfolio.

Massive electrical shortages lasting up to 18 hours a day have been caused by the absence of vital infrastructures, such as in the energy industry. The banking industry in Nepal lacks the necessary cash to fund such huge projects. Periodic banking system liquidity problems have caused loan rates to fluctuate, making investments in infrastructure projects that depend on stable rates impossible.

In addition, international organizations like the World Bank Group and Asian Development Bank stepped in because there aren't any organizations that can lend on a long-term basis with a fixed rate of interest. Nepal will gain a lot from long-term financing organizations that can increase infrastructure investment.

16.2.2 Raise Capital

Entrepreneurs in Nepal must deal with the following issues because there is no official financing available:

• The ability of entrepreneurs to get loans for their enterprises has been impeded by the absence of banks and financial institutions in many areas of the nation.

- Some businesses are unable to use this facility since the majority of banks, and institutions demand collateral— usually property and buildings—before a customer can be approved for a loan.
- There is no mechanism in place that links business owners with risk capital investors.
- Microfinance is an effective source of money for small enterprises, but it comes with high-interest rates and "lending ceilings".
- Entrepreneurs are frequently at the mercy of rogue informal lenders.

Small and medium-sized enterprises, which serve as the foundation of any economy by creating jobs, wealth, and financial stability, are most affected by these difficulties. Private equity may contribute significant value in this situation by providing the necessary risk capital injection and enhancing the balance sheets and creditworthiness of the companies.

The IFC, DFID, and private investors have recently guided startup funds in raising roughly $30 million in funding. Investment vehicles like private equity funds, however, have not been able to get a legal standing and turn into a viable asset class for the private, public, and foreign sectors to participate in due to the lack of regulatory clarity.

Private equity can assist potential entrepreneurs in accessing financing and developing the firms and organizations that will improve the region's economic and social health.

Nepal can establish the procedures necessary to get a good international credit rating through these fundamental financial sector reforms. The improvement of the banking system and private and public capital markets would encourage entrepreneurship and infrastructure expenditure and convert Nepal into an economic success story.

Political stability is signified by a robust, honest, and responsible government. It has few obstacles in pursuing the constitution's goals. However, the penetration of special interest groups into the polity from both inside and outside can easily tarnish its impartial performance, impoverish the populace whether the country is resource-rich or resource-scarce, and cause compound sclerosis to rear its ugly head, crushing any appearance of political stability. These special interest organizations serve as potent tools for lobbyists yet also fuel unfavorable feelings among the public and the polity. They have assisted in the development of Nepali political parties, rendered their differences in policy indistinguishable, and changed the focus of the country's priorities.

The public appeal of prominent party leaders is being diminished by critical media's open sponsorship of doubt about their ability to lead Nepalis through tough times and collusion with interest groups. The static nature of the human condition can only be accurately seen by logical leaders who possess a deep reservoir of bravery, confidence, and grit, as well as solid public policy ideas and craftsmanship. The Nepali people's need for basic necessities, an improvement in social and economic indicators, and a careful relaxation of geopolitical balance are all necessary for the country's crisis to be resolved. The goal of the Nepali government is to meet the reasonable requirements of the populace and link freedom, peace, and public order.

Given the delicate strategic topography, maintaining the country's correct orientation to a fluctuating regional and global balance of power becomes crucial. In order for Nepal to exercise its right to free will and utilize it to project its sovereign identity, non-alignment is now seen as a necessary component of a workable policy as a result of the world's increasing multiploidization. It can eliminate the foreign policy schizophrenia that has prevented the country from acting in adaptive behavior.

16.2.3 Policy paralysis

The article written by Dev Raj Dahal for The Rising Nepal[124], says policy paralysis in making comprehensive progress, leaders' frenzied

---

124 https://risingnepaldaily.com/news/13982

competition to secure special privileges for one's own group or party in the elections, and the lack of a common past and shared future in the pursuit of the public good, Nepal's political system is forever shifting from one set of coalition politics to the next without creating a safe and secure political space for governance. As long as Nepali leaders do not ensure the integrity of each institution, exclusively rely on the legal- rational authority derived from periodic elections, and fail to develop their legitimacy and authority from the provision of public goods and services to the population, the nation's deeply entrenched patronage system, dysfunctional public institutions, and partisan constitutional bodies will not be able to rope political stability and justice.

Nepali leaders must devise innovative, dynamic strategies to counter the tides of rising personal insecurity that are ingrained in their own habits and ways of life in order to escape the politics of static infirmity. The establishment's shared mentality and tacit agreement to maintain its hold on power through an all-party process for a long time appear to be dissolving right now, leaving them with the constitution as their sole tool to steer the government in a stable direction.

To capture the indications of political stability in Nepal, a lot of characteristics are necessary. The first is faithfully carrying out the Constitution. The proclaimed virtue of constitutionalism is to preserve the rights of people and make their lives better and more inclusive than before. It is feasible if leadership honestly upholds and puts into practice constitutionalism's core values. Likewise, funds and public policies are allotted for this purpose. To protect everyone's freedom, however, the accompanying obligations to rights must have an enforcing nature. These values guard against the tyranny of the powerful class, narrow interests, and predators, and they lead Nepali politics in the directions dictated by the state's directive principles and policies.

The primary causes of contemporary political unrest are the erosion of the state's monopoly of power, the unethical actions of wealthy elites, political class impunity, and a general lack of constitutional discipline. People's rights to life and popular sovereignty call for their own self-determination in topics that concern them, which is a requirement of civic ability to provide a good life and dignity. Civic education is a noble technique to ensure that Nepali society will always examine which worldview would be comfortable and reasonable in the views of the greater world.

The second is maintaining the division of powers and the checks and balances of the institutions of the polity and the state so that the dark side of human nature cannot overthrow institutional order, which is essential to distributing safety, wealth, and respect to individuals in a fair manner. This enables the democratic management of shared ambitions for the well-being of all Nepalis. It is necessary to retain their institutional autonomy and demarcate the jurisdiction to escape specific degrees of institutional stress produced either by overload, lack of capacity to fulfill specialist obligations or pursuing decentralized activities of multi-level governance. Although it seeks a ritualized public hearing of judges, ambassadors, and other executive functionaries, the legislature in Nepal only serves as a continuation of party politics and does little to represent the general will of the populace. In contrast, the executive in Nepal appears to stifle the independence of the judiciary. It cannot escape the command and control structure of party politics, the parliamentary whip, expulsion, and other disciplinary actions to punish lawmakers unless its specialized committees are well-equipped with expertise pertinent to policy. They are unable to act on their conscience and convictions in the service of national interests and allay unwarranted worries in such a situation.

The only remaining hope is for the vibrant public sphere, which is made up of a critical mass of Nepalis and the media, to spark discussion and debate on Nepali politics, law, leadership, economy, political culture, and foreign policy outside of the purview of special interest groups courting politicians to advance their agendas. The third is the frequent agreement inside the party to amend the constitution to reflect the zeal of the leadership or to excuse their arbitrary, unlawful actions. They have undermined the legitimacy of Nepali politics, damaged the rule of law, and fueled the ambition of the wealthy to disregard the law.

The Nepali judiciary has persistently stood in matters of citizenship, crucial national concerns, and defense of the constitution despite several inadequacies in the meticulous administration of justice and appeals for its changes, including redefining the judicial council. The life, liberty, and property of individuals are not protected by the functioning democracy in Nepal due to lax constitutional protections and selective constitutional implementation. Political instability will continue to be stoked by leaders whose conduct sets an example for their cadres and supporters to follow when the unwritten law of self-interest in money drives them in the traditional style of politics rather than the written political spirit of the constitution and party laws.

The fourth is escaping the snare of factional politics that is leader-centered. In the country, the cult of leadership worship by cadres and their party-focused media has flourished as a way to appeal to deep emotional drives for reverence to their all-pervasive authority and win favor for lucrative rewards. To appeal to their bias and broaden their political base, leaders now need complete obedience from their cadres and followers. However, such uniformity dulls people's democratic consciousness, making it harder for them to challenge their leaders about important responsibilities in promoting policies that are crucial to shared concerns supporting democratic principles. Political party institutionalization has been hampered in terms of philosophy, program, structure, and leadership succession.

People are already being exposed to crisis socialization analogous to Sri Lanka since the country has wasted valuable resources on pointless endeavors, amassed a large number of unpaid bills, and is overburdened with debt and dependency. The Nepali people are growing increasingly anxious to find a way out of the worst-case situation. Because of their habit-driven leadership style and not because of social learning, the current leaders will continue to give room for dissidents' discontent and encourage the conservative force, independent figures, and those looking for credible political alternatives claiming to represent the will of the country and the people.

16.2.4 Primordial fear

Nepal continues to experience a state of innate fear and requires deficiencies. People continue to seek economic stability, money, and a respectable way of living. They travel overseas in great numbers without placing any confidence in the national leadership.

It may be resolved by carefully managing economic life through productive endeavors, employment, education, and other necessary public services. Leaders shouldn't leave everything up to market forces that prioritize order above personal fulfillment and the survival of the fittest. They shouldn't let civil society handle the lucrative domains of political activism. They lack synchronization and are too diversified. Business should not be trusted with handling it since it is more focused on the rationalization of profit than patriotism.

Additionally, they cannot leave the big-picture considerations of policy, legislation, coordination, and collective action to the careerist bureaucracy, which is unable to begin doing enormous nation-building tasks to which they are not willing to selflessly dedicate. It maintains a paternalistic viewpoint of the Nepali people as a source of giving rather than a source of sovereignty. A semblance of political stability may be achieved by integrating all of these players into a constitutional framework, educating them about their constitutional responsibilities, and helping them understand the objectives of governance.

Full constitutional awareness among Nepalis can help them overcome their many issues, heal their illnesses, address corrective and redistributive justice for the least privileged, realize their vision for an egalitarian society, and move their country closer to both the constitutional and historical goals of democratic stability and progress.

CONCLUSION

It's somewhat true that Nepal is a developing nation with a weak infrastructure, as can be seen from the living standards of the populace. The Nepalese are not impoverished, despite the fact that Nepal is seen and acknowledged as a poor country. They have a lavish and affluent lifestyle. Because there wasn't a lot of skilled labor available in ancient times, talking about the past might help explain attitudes and obligations. As Nepal is landlocked, there is no import of any raw products.

The nation has relied on output from other sources. Natural tourism and natural evolution are celebrated in Nepal. But as time goes on, the Nepalese government is demonstrating its desire for a revolution in development with regard to incremental growth in Nepalese tourism. The country's economy has begun to show some typical changes in the upward direction, and the construction of infrastructure is progressing quickly as well. There are several businesses that work under contract with the Nepali government. The Nepalese administration is like a football game where players are often changed. The way the legislation and system are run and circulated is not fixed.

The Nepalese government has a perspective that likewise rejects the idea of wealth sharing. There is the monopoly and power system. Those who have power can demonstrate and overpower anyone. However, people who lack influence are prevented from using their legal right to remark because of the danger. There are numerous incidents of unlawful corruption and games occasionally displayed to the public, which are not carefully monitored by the government and the police.

Government officials and political leaders have also petted criminals like pets. The remittances that Nepalese young send by wasting their hard work and sweat abroad are what drive the nation's economy. Since they provide the rewards and the sources from which they and their family are able to survive, they are the nation's builders and catalysts of country growth, but because of unemployment, they are forced to squander and utilize their thoughts and hands in a foreign country.

Distinct people have different personalities; some are unpatriotic. There are many people who consider themselves to be patriotic and are investing money and their hands in the Nepalese market, and some of them are so avaricious that we also refer to them as being unpatriotic. These people have a strong focus on money; therefore, they present and go to places where they can make big money. However, the government must also work to prepare young people for employment and usefulness. The government is also acting like a deaf and dumb person by ignoring the voice and suffering of the youth.

So occasionally, it happens that graduate students go on strike in order to get a job or get unemployment benefits. Therefore, there are several risky injections that the nation's economy is being sucked into, which may be due to both internal and foreign factors. The following list of comparable and important causes for Nepal's underdevelopment includes:

1. Political instability:

Numerous types of economic ups and downs have been observed in the nation as a result of the lack of political stability and consistency, which demonstrates the impacts on the nation and its citizens. Both the administration and the people of the country depend on each other for support. Therefore, it is simple to steer the country in a growing direction if the government adopts policies that are advantageous to the people. However, since the dissolution of the last constitution in Nepal in 2063, no new constitution has been established.

Elections are held to create the country's constitution; however, the first election was unsuccessful, and the country was unable to get its constitution. Second constitutional elections were held in 2068, and six years later, on Aswin 3, the parliament was able to adopt a new constitution for the nation. Unfortunately, the constitution has not been put into effect because of the opposition to it, as it did not include the rights of the vast Madhesi people, and even those rights that were granted were fraudulently obtained and taken back. Every nine months, Nepali government elects a new prime minister. The opposition's objection prevents the parliament and the administration from putting the constitution into effect.

The sun will undoubtedly rise if the nation appears capable of upholding the constitution faithfully. The actual two-thirds of the voters have not been tried by any political party. So I suppose there arise numerous misunderstandings and mischief in the argument of pushing various alteration pins of the constitution in the parliament. Due to the parliament's procedure being halted, the constitution and the parliament appear to have little prospect of implementation.

Therefore, it is one of the most important issues that has contributed to the underdevelopment of the country.

2. Lack of education:

As far as we are aware, instructors and leaders are not subject to any restrictions when doing tasks related to the law and the country. For example, owing to power, corruption in many areas has not even been made visible or public. Therefore, these are the poisons that are turning the nation poisonous. In order to rid the nation from poison, laws must first be implemented, crimes must not be committed, and offenders must be punished. The issues with schooling are also quite evident in remote regions.

The remote learning industry is steadily declining. No chain has been established by the government to enhance or standardize them. Additionally, the kids from the rural areas aren't showing any interest in their studies since their parents utilize them as a laborer, don't allow them enough time to study, and don't even purchase them the books and supplies they need. This is another significant factor highlighting Nepal's failing educational system. Due to the Hindu culture, Nepalese people have a strong attachment to children and love them dearly. In eastern civilizations, there is a solid method for loving one's own sons and family members, but in western societies, all of these things are meaningless and pointless because people there lead busy lives.

The customary idea of not educating the daughter very much has a negative impact on the inhabitants in rural and village areas as well. They believe that the daughter was merely intended to help with household chores like cooking and cleaning. Therefore, one aspect that is hindering the growth of the country is the idea of not teaching the daughters and children. The empowerment of women is being used and extended since women are the backbone of the nation's development. However, many individuals in Nepal are unable to attend school because of poverty or a lack of local schools. Education has not reached every citizen, but efforts are being made to link urban and rural populations.

3. Unequal distribution of health:

Every citizen of the nation should be treated equally in the eyes of the government. All citizens have a complete obligation to their nation. Fewer people in a country are highly destructive, while more people are excessively bad. Therefore, there are rules for childbirth that are both inside and outside of the established rules. When dispersing the nation's revenue, the Nepalese government does not think equally. The national revenue is not distributed equitably by the Nepali government. More income is supplied to the wealthy and distributed less to the poor, increasing both their wealth and that of the wealthy.

The distribution of income divides people into two categories and groupings. People also use the market and the products in accordance with their earnings. The high income is only created by the high investment and the more sources of revenue. According to the economist, if the national income is distributed equally, impoverished people would be able to save money and earn money from a variety of sources, making them less destitute and more economically secure and confident.

The inclination of the populace to spend and invest is used to assess the nation's economy. Only those with high incomes invest, whereas a greater proportion of those with low incomes consume. So, the country is suffering from the effects of such injection as well as the differentiation in the distribution of national revenue, which has harmed and undermined economic stability. The government should establish employment and independence as a collective goal. If the populace is wealthy, only the government will be able to collect taxes, and the nation's stock of weapons and ammunition will increase.

4. Lack of establishment of industrialization:

It is also one of the main causes of Nepal's lack of progress. The fact that Nepal does not have a sizable market and that political tyranny and order exist there discourages investors from investing there. Industrialization is the primary driver of a nation's economy toward economic growth. The nation has numerous potential sources of revenue, including a variety of plants and bushes, lumber, and other raw materials, but owing to appropriate underuse, all of these resources are rapidly disappearing. The government declares that it has no interest in farming and that such resources would be invested in order to stabilize the country.

The building of industries provides several employment opportunities to the populace, which increases Nepalese growth and drives Nepalese development. Industrialization strengthens the growth path and supports the chain's quick speed movement. Industrialization is the process of producing commodities and products locally rather than importing them, saving the country's wealth.

5. Due to the landlocked country:

Due to pressure from the two large rocks, India and China, Nepal is a country made of stone that does not even attempt to expand orbecome flexible. Since the nation has never touched a body of water, it is required to import all of its raw materials from India. Nepal must follow India's instructions and carry them out. Every manufacturing and industry in Nepal depends on raw materials from India to operate. As a result, this is one of the main reasons why foreign investors choose not to make investments in the nation, along with political pressure from the outside world.

If any of the country's borders or sides contact the sea, it becomes more reliable, and there is less of a need to link to India. As a result, the country develops extremely quickly. A landlocked nation must deal with unfaithfulness in order to grow all its sectors. The nation must move and steer in the direction of its neighbors. The nation has everything, but since there aren't any resources available to run the industry, the momentum has been stunted.

6. Lack of employment opportunities or poverty:

This is one of the primary factors that led to the unintended effects. Lack of growth affects people's living standards and lifestyles in the nation. By accepting the loan from the Asian Development Bank and responding, the nation is opposing national spending. There is, therefore, an average loan of 20,000 rupees on each Nepalese person's head. The nation is not making investments in profitable industries, nor are jobs being created to employ young people and increase their income.

This saying from Plato was, "*Good people do not need a law to tell them to act responsibly, while bad people will find a way around the laws.*" I have been wondering about this quote for a while in the context of Nepal. Why do we act irresponsibly when there are so many laws in our country? There is a law to don't drink and drive, and we do drink and drive. There is now a new law in the case of Covid-19 third wave not to gather more than 25 people for events and ceremonies, but we collect more than 25 people around for our weddings, events, and traditions. There is a law not using hundi or hawala or another medium to send money to Nepal, but we choose these channels to send money to our friends and family back home.

Also, there is a law not to use corruption to cheat ordinary people in the country, but we fool commoners every day. Examples of these can be the Omni Scandal government's corruption in collecting Covid-19 test kits and medical instruments. Airbus A330 purchase scandal, where top-level bureaucrats have been indicted for embezzlement and scandal surrounding the purchase of two Airbus jets. Lalita Niwas land scandal also involves multiple government administrations conspiring and acquiring land at cheap rates, even former prime ministers for God's Shake. No wonder Nepal is among the top 117/180 on the Transparency International index and Corruption Perception Index. Not precisely "scandal", but to use or not to use MCC, a $500 million grant for poverty, economic growth is now slowly turning into a conspiracy where all the political parties and people mandate stands divided.

The blame game flaunts the news, media, Youtube, and various other secondary channels where some of our very own people have been debating and discussing the return of King as a fatherly figure to monitor these political parties. Twenty-one years after the royal massacre, Nepal seems to live in foreign policy imbalance. Some authors argue that "all roads lead to the north" on the geopolitics of Nepal, India and China relationship, and some say on "Kathmandu Dilemma" for re-thinking Nepal-India ties. Is it so that it is the playground for the US, India, and China and the people living as citizens in it.

Bordered by China and India, Nepal is a landlocked country in South

Asia. It is situated in the Himalayas and has eight of the ten highest peaks in the world. The president is the head of state, and the prime minister is the head of government in this federal parliamentary republic.

Nepal is lagging behind even the undeveloped world when it comes to poverty. Not all hope is gone, though. Particularly in light of the current economic recovery, volunteer efforts and those of non-profit organizations have the power to significantly alter circumstances.

Almost nothing that occurs in Nepal has anything to do with planning. Targets set are not achieved. No planned expenses are incurred. The causes for the failure of planning are examined in this essay, including the lack of knowledge, the few and bad project ideas, the difficulty in scheduling foreign funding, the finance ministry's opposition, and the severely constrained ability to manage development. Particular focus is placed on the arduous process of allocating funds as well as the attempt to get around fundamental political and administrative obstacles by making surface changes to the way planning is organized.

Nepal has been making great progress toward success. For the first time in decades, Nepal is in a position to dream big and implement a long-term vision that includes more and better services and opportunities for people thanks to a stable government and an ambitious economic plan. Nepal needs to diversify its financial sources. Nepal requires more funding than its administration and its development partners, including the World Bank Group, can provide.

Is the philosopher Plato remarkably astute in making such an observation in the context of Nepal? So who are the good people and the country's bad people? Are we as citizens good people who are also finding ways of getting around the law, or can the people we elected be considered good people who also find many possible ways to twist the rules we asked them to make? Perhaps it is good to forget about "Propersours Nepal" and be "Happy Nepali" instead because smiling is in our guts, and we can always find a way around the laws in some innovative and effective ways.

Congratulations on finishing the book. I hope you've enjoyed it. The growth of entrepreneurship is essential for Nepal to succeed in the future. However, there are too many hurdles and impediments, which have resulted in an unfriendly business climate. The government, the private sector, and the entrepreneurs themselves must all join together and make a concerted effort to establish an atmosphere conducive to the growth of entrepreneurship. The government should simplify the legislation and regulations and support activities such as startup financing, training, and educational opportunities for young people and entrepreneurs.

Political stability and the reduction of corruption would facilitate the entry of new entrepreneurs and the seamless operation of current ones. In the same manner, individuals should believe in the entrepreneurial spirit and be willing to take risks for the greater good of society rather than just looking for the quickest and most convenient route to personal gain. Youths should make use of the few years after college to explore, learn, and take risks in their entrepreneurial skills rather than rushing to travel overseas right after graduation. Parents should also encourage their children. In addition, entrepreneurs who have experienced all of these difficulties and possibilities should share their expertise with young people who are just starting.

Newcomers will benefit from hearing about other people's experiences and tales of success and failure. As one entrepreneur begins their road to success, they should inspire many others by their actions. Using this approach, we will be able to create a long-term entrepreneurial environment in Nepal. I am a dreamer, and like any dreamer, I am hoping that by reading this book, we will have a prosperous Nepal, and hopefully, we all can strive to make Nepal successful in innovative and intuitive ways.

Notes

Acharya, Suman. "Political Economy of Law: Issues and Extant in Contemporary Nepal." Available at SSRN 3254025 (2018).

Acemoglu, D., & Robinson, J. A. (2012). Why Nations Fail: The origins of power, prosperity, and poverty. Currency.

Adhikari, Dipak Bahadur, et al. "Challenges in transformation of informal business sector towards formal business sector in Nepal: Evidence from descriptive cross-sectional study." Asian Journal of Agricultural Extension, Economics & Sociology 39.2 (2021): 95-106.

Ashesh Shrestha, The Himalayan Times, Dec 23, 2018. Difficulties in Starting a Business in Nepal - Samriddhi Foundation. https://samriddhi.org/news-and-updates/difficulties-in-starting-a-business-in-nepal/

Bhatta, Guna Raj, et al. "Testing for uncovered interest parity conditions in a small open economy: A state space modelling approach." (2021).

Badal, Bharat Prasad. "Tourism: Visit Nepal 2020." Research Nepal Journal of development Studies 2.2 (2019): 12-32.

Birendra, K. C., Adity Dhungana, and Tek B. Dangi. "Tourism and the sustainable development goals: Stakeholders' perspectives from Nepal." Tourism Management Perspectives 38 (2021): 100822.

Bhatnagar, Stuti, and Zahid Shahab Ahmed. "Geopolitics of landlocked states in South Asia: a comparative analysis of Afghanistan and Nepal." Australian Journal of International Affairs 75.1 (2021): 60-79.

Bista, Dor Bahadur. Fatalism and development: Nepal's struggle for modernization. Orient Blackswan, 1991.

Basnet, Chudamani. "Relition or political institutions? Revisiting Dor Bahadur Bista's Fatalism and Development Thesis." Studies in Nepali History & Society 23.1 (2018): 33-58.

Bista, Dipendra Bahadur, and Anjay Kumar Mishra. "Bidding Trend and its Effects in Implementation on Road Projects of Division Road Offices of Department of Roads, Nepal." Int J Adv Res Civil Stru Engr 2.1 (2019): 1-9.

Baral, Madhab Prasad. "Changing Patterns of Migration in Nepal." Janapriya Journal of Interdisciplinary Studies 10.01 (2021): 168-177.

Bay of Bengal Initiative for Multi-Sectoral Technical and Economic Cooperation https://commerce.gov.in/international-trade/trade-agreements/indias-current-engagements-in-rtas/bay-of-bengal-initiative-for-multi-sectoral-technical-and-economic-cooperation-bimstec-free-trade-agreement-fta-negotiations-as-of-july-2014/

Chaudhary, Arbind. "Landlockedness, Corruption, and Economic Growth in BIMSTEC." (2021).

Chatterjee, Ranit, and Kenji Okazaki. "Household livelihood recovery after 2015 Nepal earthquake in informal economy: case study of shop owners in Bungamati." Procedia engineering 212 (2018): 543-550.

Calì, Massimiliano, et al. "Integrating border regions: connectivity and competitiveness in South Asia." World Bank Policy Research Working Paper 6987 (2014).

Crossette, Barbara. "Nepal: The politics of failure." World Policy Journal 22.4 (2005): 69-76.

Chamlagai, Abi. "Nepal: Terai/madhesh movements and political elites." Journal of Asian and African Studies 56.4 (2021): 949-963.

33209-013: Community-Managed Irrigated Agriculture Sector Project. https://www.adb.org/sites/default/files/project-document/81177/33209-013-iee-01.pdf

Deraniyagala, Sonali. "The political economy of civil conflict in Nepal." Oxford Development Studies 33.1 (2005): 47-62.

Dhakal, Arun, and Rajesh Kumar Rai. "Who Adopts Agroforestry in a Subsistence Economy?—Lessons from the Terai of Nepal." Forests 11.5 (2020): 565.

Deshar, Bashu Dev. "An overview of agricultural degradation in Nepal and its impact on economy and environment." Global Journal of economic and social development 3.1 (2013): 1-20.

Dhakal, Rebat Kumar. "The politics of education policymaking in Nepal." Dhakal, RK (2019). The politics of education policymaking in Nepal. Journal of Education and Research 9.1 (2019): 1-12.

Dizon, Felipe, Zetianyu Wang, and Prajula Mulmi. "The Cost of a Nutritious Diet in Bangladesh, Bhutan, India, and Nepal." (2021).

Economy, N. (2008). NEPAL RASTRA BANK. Occasional Paper, (20).

Economy Investment and Trade - Embassy of Nepal - Tokyo, Japan. https://jp.nepalembassy.gov.np/economy-investment-trade/

Even the Himalayas Have Stopped Smiling: Climate Change, Poverty and....... https://www.oxfam.org/en/research/even-himalayas-have-stopped-smiling-climate-change-poverty-and-adaptation-nepal

Education in Nepal - WENR. https://wenr.wes.org/2018/04/education-in-nepal

Fisher, James F. Trans-Himalayan traders: economy, society, and culture in northwest Nepal. Motilal Banarsidass Publishe, 1987.

Gautam, Rajeeb, Sumit Baral, and Sunil Herat. "Biogas as a sustainable energy source in Nepal: Present status and future challenges." Renewable and Sustainable Energy Reviews 13.1 (2009): 248-252.

Gnangnon, Sèna Kimm. "Internet and tax reform in developing countries." Information Economics and Policy 51 (2020): 100850.

Hatlebakk, Magnus. "Nepal: A political economy analysis." Report (2017).

IHP-VIII: Water Security - UNESCO. https://en.unesco.org/themes/water-security/hydrology/IHP-VIII-water-security

History of marijuana strains - Blog Alchimia Grow Shop. https://www.alchimiaweb.com/blogen/marijuana-growing-guide/history-of-marijuana-strains/

How will Nepal develop in the next decade? | Nepali Times. https://www.nepalitimes.com/banner/how-will-nepal-develop-in-the-next-decade/

Joshi, Toyanath, et al. "Nepal at the edge of sword with two edges: The COVID-19 pandemics and sustainable development goals." Journal of Agriculture and Food Research 4 (2021): 100138.

Johnson, Andrew, et al. "Nepal: a country where water policy is in flux." Water Markets. Edward Elgar Publishing, 2021.

Karki, Dipendra. "The dynamic relationship between tourism and economy: Evidence from Nepal." Journal of Business and Management 5 (2018): 16-22.

Karki, Shova Thapa, and Mirela Xheneti. "Formalizing women entrepreneurs in Kathmandu, Nepal: Pathway towards empowerment?." International Journal of Sociology and Social Policy (2018).

Kutal, Durga, et al. "Factors that influence the plant use knowledge in the middle mountains of Nepal." PloS one 16.2 (2021): e0246390.

Karki, D., Upreti, S., Bhandari, U., Rajbhandari, S., Devkota, N., Parajuli, S., & Paudel, U. R. (2021). Does the Formal Financial Sector Enhance Small Business Employment Generation in Nepal: Evidence from Cross-Sectional Data. Journal of Social Economics Research, 8(2), 155-164.

Khadka, Jiban. "Effect of governance on educational performance in Nepal." Journal of Education and Research 11.1 (2021): 97-114.

Khadka, Jiban. "Effect of governance on educational performance in Nepal." Journal of Education and Research 11.1 (2021): 97-114.

Khanal, Saugat, and Mamata Shrestha. "Agro-tourism: Prospects, importance, destinations and challenges in Nepal." Archives of Agriculture and Environmental Science 4.4 (2019): 464-471.

Khanal, Uttam. "Contribution of Remit Economy on Poverty Reduction in Nepal." Humanit. Soc. Sci. 8 (2020): 131-142.

Katherine Loh, Nirjan Rai, Nepal Economy Hindered by Political Uncertainty, May 11, 2011, The Asia Foundation, Available from here: https://asiafoundation.org/2011/05/11/nepal-economy-hindered-by-political-uncertainty/

Knight, K. E. (1967). A descriptive model of the intra-firm innovation process. The journal of business, 40(4), 478-496.

_____, Boosting entrepreneurship: target the youth. The Himalayan Times, Vol. XX, No. 41, January 3, 2022, Available from here: https://thehimalayantimes.com/opinion/boosting-entrepreneurshiptarget-the-youth

_____. Legalise cannabis. The Himalayan Times, Vol. XX, No. 237, July 18, 2022. Available online from here: https://thehimalayantimes.com/blogs/legalise-cannabis

_____, A road block, Editorial section: Op-ed, The Kathmandu Post, Vol. XXII No. 210, page 07, Tuesday, September 16, 2014.

_____., Nepali migrant workers abroad, Editorial section: Topics, The Himalayan Times, Vol. XII No. 286, page 08, Wednesday, September 4, 2013.

_____., The great quake, Editorial section: Op-ed, The Kathmandu Post, Vol. XXIII No. 71, page 06, Thursday, April 30, 2015.

_____ Can Nepal benefit from a king?:let the people decide, Editorial section: Op-ed, The Himalayan Times, Vol. XXI, No. 100, March 02, 2023

_____ State of anomie, Editorial section: Topics, The Himalayan Times, Vol.XXI, No. 70, January 31, 2023.

Khadka, N. (1998). Challenges to developing the economy of Nepal. Contemporary South Asia, 7(2), 147-165.

Kollmair, Michael, et al. "New figures for old stories: Migration and remittances in Nepal." Migration Letters 3.2 (2006): 151-160.

Kingdoms of South Asia - Nepal. https://www.historyfiles.co.uk/KingListsFarEast/IndiaNepal.htm

Lee, Hanol, and Toure Moumbark. "Climate Change, Corruption, and Business Bribes in South Asia." Finance Research Letters (2022): 102685.

Levine, Arthur. Why innovation fails. SUNY Press, 1980.

Lord, Austin. "Speculation and seismicity: Reconfiguring the hydropower future in post-earthquake Nepal." Water, technology and the nation-state. Routledge, 2018. 167-188.

Mulmi, Amish Raj, and Bipin Ghimire. "All roads lead north: Nepal's turn to China." (2021): 154-158.

Nepal, Sanjay K. "Tourism-induced rural energy consumption in the Annapurna region of Nepal." Tourism Management 29.1 (2008): 89-100.

Nepal, Rabindra, M. Indra Al Irsyad, and Sanjay Kumar Nepal. "Tourist arrivals, energy consumption and pollutant emissions in a developing economy–implications for sustainable tourism." Tourism Management 72 (2019): 145-154.

Neopane, Abyaya, and Swarnim Waglé. "Appraisal of Global Economic Outlook in the time of COVID-19." (2020).

Nepal - SikhiWiki, free Sikh encyclopedia.. https://www.sikhiwiki.org/index.php/Nepal

Nepal - Luxury Travel Guide | ATJ. https://www.atj.com/destinations/Nepal/overview

Nepal Travel Info | Himalaya Summit Club. https://www.himalayasummitclub.com/nepal-travel-info

Nepal Economy Hindered by Political Uncertainty. https://asiafoundation.org/2011/05/11/nepal-economy-hindered-by-political-uncertainty/

Nepal: Political instability, growth, and the role of think-tanks. https://www.freiheit.org/south-asia/nepal-political-instability-growth-and-role-think-tanks

Poudyal, Ramhari, et al. "Mitigating the current energy crisis in Nepal with renewable energy sources." Renewable and Sustainable Energy Reviews 116 (2019): 109388.

Paudel, Ramesh, and Swarnim Waglé. "Structural Transformation and Growth: Whither Agriculture in Nepal?." Agricultural Transformation in Nepal. Springer, Singapore, 2019. 11-25.

Paudel, Tulsi, et al. "A macro analysis of tourist arrival in Nepal." The Journal of Asian Finance, Economics, and Business 8.1 (2021): 207-215.

Poudel, Mitra Bandhu. Nepal's Foreign Policy and Emerging Global Trends. Eds. Mohan Krishna Shrestha, and Pramod Jaiswal. GB Books, 2021.

Paudel, Dipti, Marc Jeuland, and Sunil Prasad Lohani. "Cooking-energy transition in Nepal: trend review." Clean Energy 5.1 (2021): 1-9.

Pyakuryal, B., Thapa, Y. B., & Roy, D. (2005). Trade liberalization and food security in Nepal.

Pyakuryal, Bishwambher. Nepal's development tragedy: Threats and possibilities. Fine Print, 2013.

Rana, Pashupati Shumshere JB. "India and Nepal: The political economy of a relationship." Asian Survey (1971): 645-660.

Regmi, Kapil Dev. "The political economy of 2015 Nepal earthquake: Some critical reflections." Asian geographer 33.2 (2016): 77-96.

Robinson, James A., and Daron Acemoglu. Why nations fail: The origins of power, prosperity and poverty. London: Profile, 2012.

Regmi, Kapil Dev. "The international political economy of educational policy development in Nepal: 1950-2020." Asia Pacific Journal of Education (2021): 1-16.

Regmi, Kapil Dev. "Higher education in Nepal: A handmaiden of neoliberal instrumentalism." Higher Education Policy 34.2 (2021): 393-411.

Rae, Ranjit. Kathmandu Dilemma: Resetting India-Nepal Ties. Penguin Random House India Private Limited, 2021.

Rajamohan, P. G. (2020). Nepal: State in Dilemma. In Armed Conflicts in South Asia 2008 (pp. 211-237). Routledge India.

Rai, Jayanta. "Including the excluded? The political economy of the constituency development fund in post-war Nepal." Conflict, Security & Development 21.6 (2021): 805-830.

Riaz, Ali, and Subho Basu. Paradise lost?: state failure in Nepal. Lexington Books, 2007.

Ruszczyk, Hanna A. "Newly urban Nepal." Urban Geography 42.2 (2021): 218-225.

Sharma, Kishor. "The political economy of civil war in Nepal." World Development 34.7 (2006): 1237-1253.m

Seddon, David, Jagannath Adhikari, and Ganesh Gurung. "Foreign labor migration and the remittance economy of Nepal." Critical Asian Studies 34.1 (2002): 19-40.

Sigdel, Bama Dev. "Belt and Road Initiatives: China and South Korea's Economic Ties with South Asia and Nepal." (2020).

Sarker, Tapan, Shristi Tandukar, and Sima Rani Dey. "Promoting sustainable development through realizing the demographic dividend opportunity in the digital economy: A case study of Nepal." (2021).

Steinkamp, Sven, and Frank Westermann. "Development aid and illicit capital flight: Evidence from Nepal." The World Economy (2021).

Sharma, Basu. "Socio-economic problems of remittance economy: the case of Nepal." Journal of Advanced Management Science Vol 5.4 (2017): 285-290.

Timilsina, Govinda, and Jevgenijs Steinbuks. "Economic costs of electricity load shedding in Nepal." Renewable and Sustainable Energy Reviews 146 (2021): 111112.

Tamang, Min Kumar, and Milan Shrestha. "Let me Fly Abroad: Student Migrations in the Context of Nepal." Research in Educational Policy and Management 3.1 (2021): 1-18.

Trade and Investment Opportunities in Nepal - Berlin, Germany. https://de.nepalembassy.

gov.np/trade-investment-opportunities-nepal/

Top 20 Tourist Places in Katmandu – Telegraph. https://telegra.ph/Top-20-Tourist-Places-in-Katmandu-05-30

Ujwal Thapa (2012), Why Nepal Fails? (repeatedly), Available from here: https://www.whynepal.com/governance/failed-nepal/

Vaidya, R. (2021). Relationship between stock market and economic development: A study on Nepal Stock Exchange Limited. Khowpa Journal, 4(1), 62-71.

World Bank Group. "Nepal Development Update, April 2021: Harnessing Export Potential for a Green, Inclusive, and Resilient Recovery." (2021).

Wagle, Udaya. "Reluctant privatization: assessing the higher education context and policy formation in Nepal." Educational Research for Policy and Practice (2021): 1-17.

Wagle, Swarnim, "The Great Upheaval: Resetting Development Policy and Institutions for the Decade of Action in Asia and the Pacific." Cambridge University Press, February 28, 2022 (Edited with K. Wignaraja).

Watkins, David, and Murari Regmi. "Attributing academic success and failure in Nepal." The Journal of social psychology 134.2 (1994): 241-242.

Whelpton, John. A history of Nepal. Cambridge University Press, 2005.

Xheneti, Mirela, and Shova Thapa Karki. "Transitioning into the Formal-Women Entrepreneurs in the Informal Economy of Nepal." Training (2021).

Zurick, David N. "Adventure travel and sustainable tourism in the peripheral economy of Nepal." Annals of the Association of American geographers 82.4 (1992): 608-628.

www.ingramcontent.com/pod-product-compliance
Lightning Source LLC
Chambersburg PA
CBHW050533190326
41458CB00007B/1767